The Best of *Holidays & Seasonal Celebrations* Cooking with Kids

A compilation of preK-3 issues 1-12,
preK-K issues 1-8, and grades 1-3 issues 13-21

tlc

Teaching & Learning Company
1204 Buchanan St., P.O. Box 10
Carthage, IL 62321-0010

Edited and compiled by Ellen Sussman

Cover photo by Images and More Photography

Cover design by Jennifer Morgan

Illustrations by:

Elizabeth Adams
Janet Armbrust
Cara Bradshaw
Gary Hoover
Becky Radtke
Shelly S. Rasche
Mary Galan Rojas
Christina Schofield
Veronica Terrill
Gayle Vella

ISBN No. 1-57310-260-1

Printing No. 987654321

Teaching & Learning Company
1204 Buchanan St., P.O. Box 10
Carthage, IL 62321-0010

At the time of publication every effort was made to insure the accuracy of the information included in this book. However, we cannot guarantee that agencies and organizations mentioned will continue to operate or to maintain these current locations.

This book belongs to

____

Contributors:

Carlene Americk
Carol Ann Bloom
Amanda Boor
Stephanie Brown
Jo Jo Cavalline
Marie E. Cecchini
Elaine Hansen Cleary
Donna L. Clovis
Tania Kourempis-Cowling
Teresa E. Culpeper
Rebecca Kai Dotlich
Robynne Eagan
Jo Anne O'Donnell
Kim Rankin
Patricia M. Snell
Devorah Stone
Donna Stringfellow
Ellen Sussman
Carolyn Ross Tomlin
Mary Tucker
Judy Wolfman

Recipes and Cooking Activities

Dear Teacher or Parent,

Ever since we introduced our *Holidays & Seasonal Celebrations* magazines, the cooking and recipe features have been popular favorites. Many readers, seeing creative new ideas sent in by teachers from across the country, sent us their own personal classroom favorites which expanded our collection of kid-pleasing recipes.

Cooking with kids in class, in after-school programs and even in camp is consistently popular because it's so interactive. Kids cooperate and bring in ingredients, they help to sift, mix and stir, they learn how to measure and approximate and in a short amount of time they get to see the fruits of their labor change–from single unrelated ingredients to a completed and tasty treat.

Cooking becomes even more interactive when families become involved. Preparing a recipe and inviting parents and grandparents to sample class-made treats is a wonderful culmination to share. What parent doesn't love to see their child motivated and stimulated!

From our huge collection, we've selected a very varied and wonderfully wide selection of seasonal, holiday, multicultural and food-theme recipes and cooking activities to keep you and your kids stimulated throughout the school year. We've included some fun summer surprises so cooking with your kids doesn't have to go on vacation just because it's summer!

Enjoy and bon appetit!

Sincerely,

Ellen Sussman

Ellen Sussman

If you would like to contribute to future issues of *Holidays & Seasonal Celebrations*, please direct your submissions to:

Teaching & Learning Company
Holidays & Seasonal Celebrations
1204 Buchanan St., P.O. Box 10
Carthage, IL 62321-0010

Back-to-School Treats

Use these simple, easy, and fun-to-prepare recipes to kick-start the new school year.

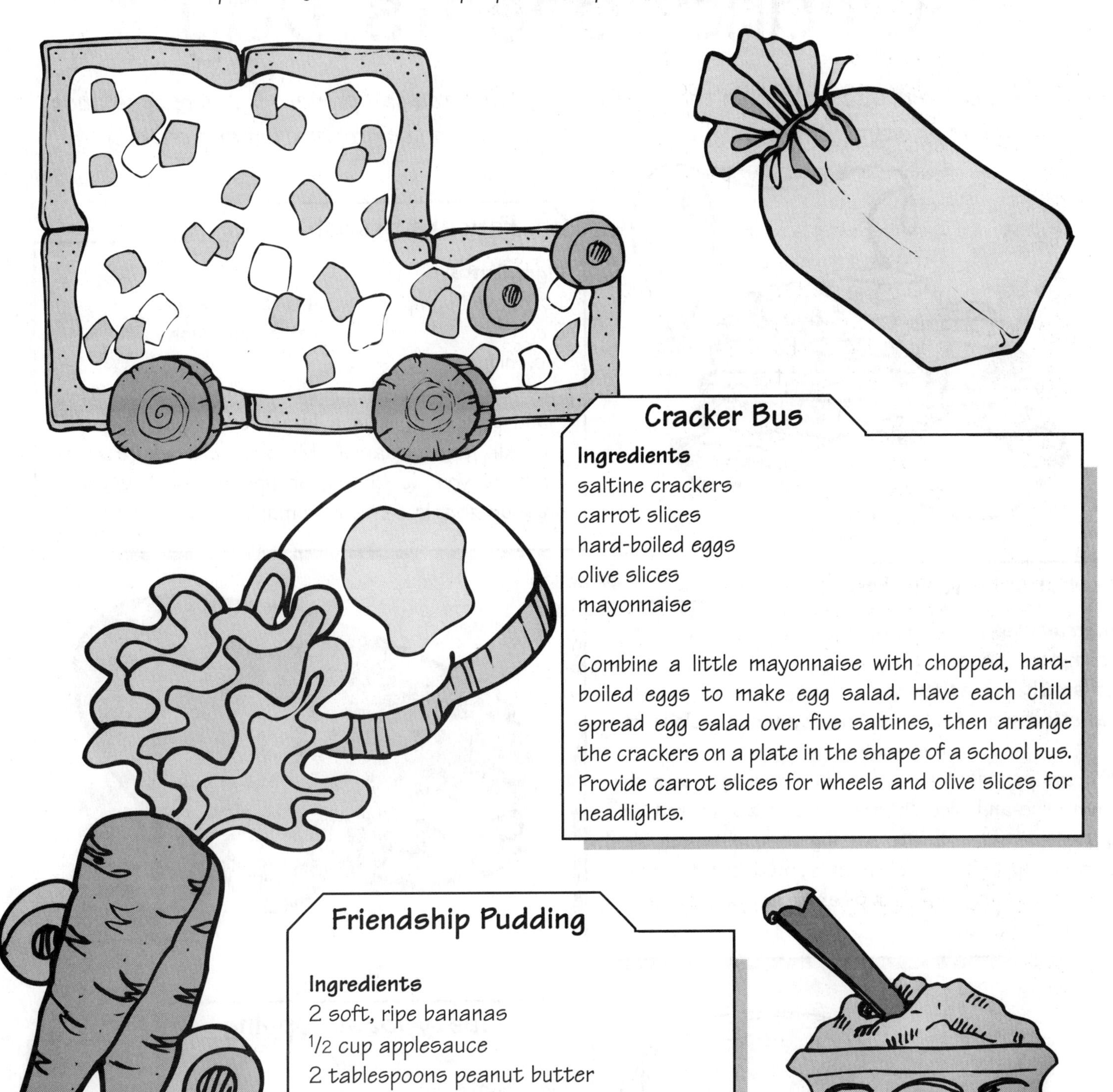

Cracker Bus

Ingredients
saltine crackers
carrot slices
hard-boiled eggs
olive slices
mayonnaise

Combine a little mayonnaise with chopped, hard-boiled eggs to make egg salad. Have each child spread egg salad over five saltines, then arrange the crackers on a plate in the shape of a school bus. Provide carrot slices for wheels and olive slices for headlights.

Friendship Pudding

Ingredients
2 soft, ripe bananas
1/2 cup applesauce
2 tablespoons peanut butter
2 tablespoons honey

Cut and mash the bananas until smooth. Stir in the applesauce, peanut butter, and honey. Beat with a wire whisk until smooth. Chill and enjoy.

Goodies for Grandparents' Day

Invite grandparents to brunch on their special day. Children can prepare these recipes ahead of time or grandparents might be delighted to join in the preparation and cooking.

Pancake Brunch

Ingredients

1 c. cooked pumpkin
2 eggs
3 c. milk
4 c. pancake mix
1 tsp. cinnamon

Place pancake mix in a large bowl. Add eggs, milk, pumpkin, and cinnamon. Mix well with a wire whisk. Cook as you would regular pancakes, on a lightly greased griddle. Serve with maple syrup or honey.

Pancake Roll-Ups

Ingredients

"complete" pancake mix
cream cheese, softened
variety of fresh fruits—berries, bananas, melons, etc.

Prepare pancakes as directed on package. Have children slice and dice the fresh fruits as desired, and place them in separate serving bowls with individual serving spoons. Let children spread cream cheese over their pancakes, add fresh fruit pieces, then roll them up and eat.

Tasty Toast Topping

Ingredients

1 cup sugar
1 tablespoon grated orange rind
1/2 cup orange juice

Thoroughly mix all of the ingredients together. Spread on toast, bread, or crackers.

Minty Orange Tea

Ingredients

6 oranges
1 lemon
1 1/2 quarts water
1/2 cup dried mint leaves
orange and lemon rind
gauze and string

Squeeze the juice from the oranges and lemon. Place the juice in a large pot. Add the water. Grate the citrus peels and crush the dried mint leaves. Place the citrus rind and the mint leaves into a piece of gauze, form a sack, and secure the sack with string. Drop the sack into the liquid in the pot. Stir the liquid and heat to boiling. Reduce the heat and simmer about 15 minutes. Cool slightly before serving. Add honey, if desired. Note: This recipe makes about 12 cups. Dried mint leaves can be found at a health food store.

A simple and fun food project to prepare ahead of time, these Peanut Butter Dippers are a great gift to present to grandparents who come to school on their special day.

Peanut Butter Dippers

Ingredients

2 c. peanut butter baking pieces
pretzel rods
toppings (flaked coconut, chopped nuts, candy sprinkles)

Melt the baking pieces in the top of a double boiler. Dip the pretzel rods into the melted morsels. Spread the melted candy over the top half of the pretzel rod with a blunt knife, then roll the warm candy section into one of the toppings. Cover two or three candy-coated pretzels with plastic wrap and tie with a decorative ribbon for a delicious Grandparents' Day gift.

Rosh Hashanah

Jewish New Year

Jewish Egg Bread – Challah

A special round-shaped bread is served on Rosh Hashanah. The round shape symbolizes the circle of life. Here is an easy, fast version of the traditional bread recipe.

Utensils

- 1 large bowl
- measuring cups and spoons
- large wooden spoons
- baking trays

Ingredients

- 2 cups warm water
- 4 tablespoons sugar
- 2 teaspoons salt
- 2 eggs
- 4 tablespoons shortening
- 2 packages or 2 tablespoons of fast-rising active dry yeast
- 4 1/2 cups all-purpose flour
- 1 beaten egg or mayonnaise

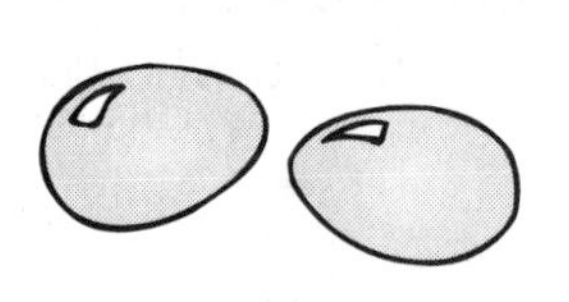

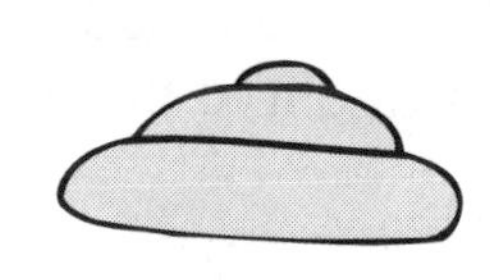

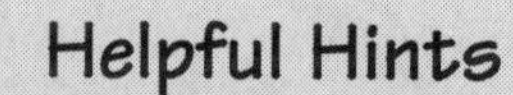

Mix together water, sugar, salt, eggs, and shortening. Add dry yeast. While stirring, pour in four cups of flour, a cup at a time.

Vigorously knead dough on floured board for at least five minutes. Dough should be smooth. Cover the dough with a wet towel or large garbage bag. Let it rise in a high place or in an unheated oven away from drafts until doubled, for about 30 or 40 minutes.

Divide dough. Give each child a portion. Have the children roll out the dough into a long "snake." Then coil the snake into a bun. (See diagram.) Spread beaten egg or mayonnaise on bun. Let rise for a half an hour and put in 400°F oven. Or let the children take the dough home and bake it there. Refrigeration retards the rising process.

by Devorah Stone

Helpful Hints

- Check the date on the fast-rising dry yeast.
- Quarter cups are easier than whole cups for small hands.
- Knead the dough to lively music.
- Dough can be put in a refrigerator overnight and then used the next morning.
- You can freeze it after the first rising and thaw it out to use the next day.
- How fast dough rises depends on your altitude and the moisture and temperature of the air as well as the type of yeast used.
- Optional: Add 1 cup raisins when kneading the dough. Sprinkle poppy seeds on top after shaping the dough.

Honey Applesauce Mixture

Ingredients

- applesauce
- honey or sugar and cinnamon
- maple syrup, finely ground nuts, yogurt, raisins (optional)
- bread or crackers

Put out bowls with different ingredients. Let the children mix applesauce with the honey, sugar and cinnamon, and so on. Then let children spread the mixture on bread or crackers.

Honey Cake

Ingredients

2 eggs, beaten
1/4 cup (60 ml) coffee
1 3/4 cup (420 ml) sifted flour
1/2 tsp. (2.5 ml) baking soda
1/2 cup (120 ml) chopped walnuts
1/2 cup (120 ml) sugar
1 T. (15 ml) oil
3/4 t. (3.75 ml) baking powder
2 T. (30 ml) warm honey
1 standard size loaf pan

Add sugar to eggs, beat until light and fluffy. Mix coffee, honey and oil together and combine with eggs. Sift flour, baking powder and baking soda. Add nuts and egg mixture to batter, stirring constantly. Pour batter into greased loaf pan and bake at 350°F (175°C) for 45 minutes. Allow to cool. Cut the honey cake according to how many pieces you will need.

Keeping Afloat

Activity

This October, official Popcorn Poppin' Month, let popcorn help your students better understand the concept of density. Begin by displaying popcorn in both its cooked and uncooked forms. Invite several students to place one of each variety into a cup of water, observe, and comment on the results. They will note that the kernel sinks, while the puff floats. Help them to conclude that the puffed piece floats because it is less dense, or less compact, than the kernel. Next, try dropping a few kernels into a glass of soda water or ginger ale. The kernels will sink; then carbonated gas bubbles will surround them, lifting them to the surface. The bubbles will break upon reaching the surface of the liquid, and the kernels will sink again. Help students to conclude that the bubbles help the kernels to become less dense.

All or Nothing

Activity

Pop some corn with your students. They will observe that most, but not all, of the kernels puffed. Popcorn puffs because there is moisture within each kernel that turns to steam when the kernels are heated. The steam expands until it breaks the sides of the kernel open. Experiment with the unpopped kernels to see if you can get them to pop. Place the unpopped kernels in a jar and cover them with water. Let them stand for 5-10 minutes. Remove them from the water and try popping them once again. This time they should pop. What conclusions can your students draw from this experiment?

Marshmallow Raisin Popcorn Treats

Sweet and sticky, this popcorn pleaser will be ideal for kids to also try at home.

Ingredients

1/2 cup butter or margarine
1 bag mini marshmallows (10 1/2 oz. size)
1/4 cup honey
1 cup raisins
1/2 cup popcorn kernels to yield 10 cups popped popcorn
vegetable oil cooking spray

Pop popcorn prior to preparing recipe. Melt butter or margarine in frying pan. Reduce heat to low and add marshmallows. Stir constantly until marshmallows are completely melted. Add honey and continue to stir well. When honey is completely mixed in, remove frying pan from burner. Let mixture cool for about five minutes. Add mixture to bowl of popped popcorn. Add raisins, stirring completely making sure everything is well coated. Spray vegetable oil onto a cookie sheet. Pour popcorn mixture onto the sheet pressing mixture down firmly. Allow to set on cookie sheet for about two hours. Cut into squares and serve.

Popular Pizza Treats

Pizza Roll-Ups

Ingredients

pita bread
tomato or pizza sauce
cheese slices

Slice each pita in half to make two "rounds." Spoon and spread warmed tomato or pizza sauce over the pita half. Tear a cheese slice into pieces and set into the sauce. Begin at one end of the pita pizza and roll it into a cylinder. These can be eaten as is or placed in a hot oven (or toaster oven) for a few minutes, just to warm through. Additional toppings may be added if you choose.

Pizza-Flavored Popcorn

Ingredients

2 qts. popped corn
1/2 tsp. garlic salt
1 tsp. oregano
1/4 c. margarine
1/2 tsp. table salt
1/2 c. Parmesan cheese

Combine margarine, salts, and oregano in a small saucepan. Stir over low heat until margarine melts. Pour the mixture over the popped corn and mix well. Spread popcorn in a shallow pan and sprinkle with cheese.

Bike Wheel Pizza

Ingredients

English muffins
cheese strips
pizza sauce
pepperoni

Spoon and spread pizza sauce (or tomato sauce) on a muffin half. Place thin cheese strips radiating from the center of the muffin like the spokes of a bike wheel. Add a slice of pepperoni in the center. Place in an oven or toaster oven until the cheese melts.

Make another version of this snack that needs no cooking: Bike Wheel Rice Cakes. Spread peanut butter on a rice cake. Add pretzel stick or carrot stick spokes. Place a banana slice or several raisins in the center.

Sailboat Snacks

Invite your youngsters to create a special snack for one of autumn's many celebrations.

Columbus Day Breakfast Boats

Ingredients
apples, halved and cored
strawberry yogurt
bread slices, toasted

Set an apple half on a plate, curved side down. Fill the center of the apple half with straw-berry yogurt. Cut a triangle shape from a slice of toast. Insert the toast triangle into the yogurt for a sail.

Tuna Boat Melts

Ingredients
bread slices
cheese slices
tuna fish, drained
mayonnaise

Lightly toast the bread slices. Combine the mayonnaise with the tuna to make tuna salad. Spread tuna salad over the bread slices. Use blunt knives to cut cheese into triangles and half circles. Place one of each shape on the tuna salad in the shape of a sailboat, adding a small cheese rectangle to connect the two. Place the open-faced sandwiches under a broiler or in a toaster oven just long enough to melt the cheese. Cool slightly before eating.

Festive and Fun Recipes for Fall

A"maize"ing Popcorn Balls

Ingredients

1 1/2 c. uncooked popcorn
1 small box orange-flavored gelatin
1 c. sugar
1 c. light corn syrup
orange food coloring
margarine

Pop the corn kernels and set aside. Have the children measure the gelatin, sugar, corn syrup, and a few drops of food coloring into a saucepan. Heat this mixture to a full boil. Pour the orange syrup over the popped corn, and have the children use wooden spoons to stir the combination until the popcorn is thoroughly coated. Allow the popcorn to cool. Provide the children with sheets of waxed paper to use as working surfaces, and help them coat their hands with a thin layer of margarine. Let them shape a small amount of orange popcorn into a ball. Store the individual balls in plastic wrap or plastic sandwich bags until ready to eat.

Cool Fondue

Ingredients

applesauce
vanilla yogurt
fresh fruit pieces
cinnamon
ground cloves
nutmeg

Combine equal amounts of applesauce and yogurt. Mix well. For each cup of applesauce used, stir in 1 tsp. of cinnamon and 1/4 tsp. of ground cloves. Sprinkle the top with nutmeg. To eat, dip pieces of fresh fruit into the mixture. Toothpicks are optional.

Pumpkin Spice Pudding

Ingredients

1 c. cooked pumpkin
1/4 tsp. cinnamon
1/4 tsp. ground cloves
1 T. honey
1/4 tsp. salt
1 1/2 c. milk
1 small box vanilla instant pudding

Have the children measure and combine the pumpkin, honey, salt, cinnamon, and ground cloves in a mixing bowl. Stir in the milk and mix well. Add the instant pudding and beat with a wire whisk until the mixture begins to thicken, about 1 minute. Chill before serving.

Candied Nuts

Ingredients
1 cup shelled nuts (your choice)
4 tablespoons sugar
4 tablespoons honey

Mix all of the ingredients together. Stir well to completely coat the nuts with the sugar/honey mixture. Spread the mixture out on a cookie sheet. Bake at 350° for about 10 minutes. Carefully transfer the hot, candied nuts to waxed paper and cool. Eat them warm, or refrigerate them to eat chilled.

Warm Fuzzy Punch

Ingredients
1 qt. apple cider
1 c. orange juice
1/2 c. lemon juice
1/2 c. pineapple juice
1 cinnamon stick
1/2 tsp. ground cloves
honey (optional)

Combine all ingredients in a large crock pot or slow cooker. Heat through and simmer for 10 minutes before serving. Serve warm. Add honey to sweeten, if desired.

Orange Yogurt Pops

Ingredients
1 quart vanilla yogurt
1 large can frozen orange juice
1 tablespoon vanilla
1/4 cup honey

Mix the yogurt with the orange juice. Add the vanilla and honey. Mix well and pour into small paper cups. Add a craft stick to each cup. Freeze. To serve, run the pops under hot tap water until they loosen from the cups.

Pumpkin Frosties

Ingredients
vanilla ice cream, softened
cooked pumpkin
milk
cinnamon
plastic cups
plastic spoons

Provide the children with individual cups and spoons for making their own frosty pumpkin drinks. Help them place one scoop of ice cream, 1 tablespoon of cooked pumpkin, 1/2 cup of milk, and a sprinkle of cinnamon into their cups. Have them mix the ingredients thoroughly to make a creamy pumpkin-flavored drink.

Pumpkin Parfait

Ingredients
orange sherbet
chocolate wafer fingers
Smarties™ or Reese's Pieces™
(broke into little bits)
chocolate/butterscotch chips
bowls (dessert size)
whipping cream
ice cream scoop

Have each student spoon a large, rounded scoop of orange sherbet into a dessert dish. Gently push the end of a chocolate wafer cookie into the top of the ice cream, far enough to keep it from falling over; this is the pumpkin's stem. Push chocolate or butterscotch chips into the front of the ice cream for the pumpkin's eyes. (If you put the pointed end into the ice cream, they stick easily.) Add more chips for the mouth. Spoon some whipping cream all around the pumpkin. Sprinkle crushed bits of Smarties™ or Reese's Pieces™ on top of the cream. Smile and enjoy!

Orange Pumpkin Salad

Ingredients

cottage cheese
celery chunks
tangerine or mandarin orange slices

Pat a mound of cottage cheese into a circle shape on a plate. Arrange several citrus slices on the cottage cheese in the shape of a pumpkin. Add a celery chunk stem.

Mini Cereal Cakes

Ingredients

2/3 cup butter or margarine
1/3 cup golden corn syrup
1 cup sunflower seeds or chopped nuts
2/3 cup raisin bran cereal, slightly crushed
orange food coloring

Melt the butter and corn syrup in a sauce-pan over low heat. Add several drops of food coloring. Remove the pan from the heat. Stir in the cereal and the seeds or nuts. Mix well. Spoon out onto waxed paper, cool, and serve.

Healthful Pumpkin Seed Snacks

Ingredients

washed pumpkin seeds (scooped from a fresh pumpkin)
2 T. salt
4 cups water
oil for cookie sheet

Dissolve the salt in the water. Add the clean pumpkin seeds and soak for 1 1/2 to 2 hours. Pat the seeds dry and spread them evenly on a lightly oiled cookie sheet. Bake at 225°F for 1/2 to 1 hour, or until golden brown and crunchy. Allow to cool before handling. Good, and good for you!

Marshmallow Sandwich

Ingredients

round crackers
cream cheese
food coloring (red, green, yellow, orange)
miniature marshmallows

Add a couple of drops of food coloring to cream cheese; mix with a spoon until blended. Spread the cheese over a round cracker. Put several mini marshmallows on top. Spread some cheese on a second cracker. Place on top of marshmallows, cheese side down, to complete your sandwich. Bite down and enjoy!

Chocolate Leaves

Ingredients

semisweet chocolate baking squares
waxed paper
fresh leaves (assorted)
double boiler

Put a leaf between two sheets of waxed paper and place on a cookie sheet. In a double boiler, melt the chocolate. Pour over leaf. Refrigerate for several hours. Peel off waxed paper from cooled chocolate. You should have a fine imprint of your leaf. Have your leaf and eat it, too.

Fall Fantasy

Ingredients

gelatin powder (orange, green, red, yellow)
Styrofoam™ cups or clear plastic cups
spearmint leaf-shaped jelly candies (optional)
extra large bowl
mint leaves (fresh)
mixing spoon

Have the children make the gelatin, one flavor at a time, using an extra large bowl. Mix each new flavor into the previous one and stir. Once all four colors are mixed, pour into individual clear, plastic glasses or Styrofoam™ cups. Refrigerate until set. Just before serving, add a fresh mint leaf or spearmint leaf jelly candy to each cup.

I like to use the clear plastic cups so the children can see their mixed fall colors. They love the different tastes.

A variation is to make a Rainbow Fantasy. Make one color each day, pouring it into the clear glasses, then refrigerating. The next day add a second color, and so on, until you have a rainbow. The reactions are worth the time.

Orange Juice Cupcakes

Ingredients

1 c. orange juice
1 egg
2 c. flour, divided
1/3 c. salad oil
1 pkg. yeast
1/2 tsp. salt
2/3 c. plus 1 T. honey
1 tsp. vanilla

Heat the orange juice in a saucepan until warm. Remove from heat and stir in the yeast, 1 tablespoon of honey, and 1 cup of flour. Set aside until mixture is warm and bubbly, about 10-15 minutes. Meanwhile, place the egg in a bowl and beat until foamy. Stir in the salad oil, 2/3 cup of honey, 1 cup of flour, salt, and vanilla. Add the bubbly yeast mixture to the bowl. Place the batter in muffin papers or greased muffin cups and allow to rise 40 minutes in a 150°F oven. Then increase the oven temperature to 350°F and bake the cupcakes for 20 minutes.

Frosting and Decorating

Mix confectioners' sugar with a small amount of milk until you reach a spreadable consistency. Stir in a few drops of orange food coloring and a few drops of orange extract. Frost cooled cupcakes. Turn each cupcake into a jack-o'-lantern by adding candy corn facial features and a green jelly-candy stem.

Colorful Autumn Crackers

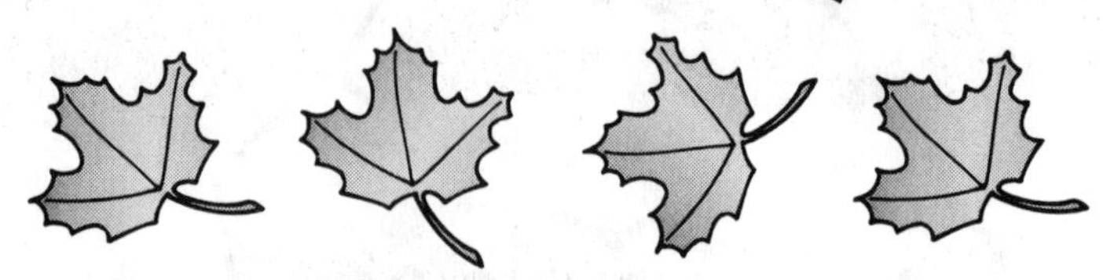

Red, yellow, and brown,

Leaves are falling all over town.

In fall there are many colors to see,

Let's make some colors! It's as easy as
1-2-3.

We'll start with three colors—red,
yellow, and blue,

After mixing, we'll have the colors—
orange, green, and purple, too!

Learning about colors will be fun.

We'll also have a treat to eat when we
are done.

Materials

- pretzel sticks
- marshmallow creme
- food coloring
- paper plates
- graham crackers

Directions

1. Using a pencil, "slice" your paper plate like a pizza until you have six slices.
2. Place a dab of marshmallow creme on every other slice.
3. Drop red food coloring on the first dab, yellow on the second, and blue food coloring on the last.
4. Using a different pretzel stick for each color, mix coloring into creme.
5. Now you are ready to mix colors. Using pretzel sticks, mix two colors together, in the "slice" between them.
6. Spread colorful creme on crackers.

When we started, the colors we had
were only three,

But after mixing colors, what did you
see?

Mixing red and yellow made orange—
but we were not through.

Red and blue would make purple;
green was made with yellow and
blue.

In fall you see many colors as you walk
down the street,

But we made some colors into a snack
that we could eat.

by Stephanie Brown

Fall Is the Time for APPLES

Apples are one of the most popular fruits in the world! They are tasty, beautiful, and full of vitamins and minerals that keep us healthy.

It is said that the Romans brought apples to England, where they were grown. When the English came to America in 1629, they brought apple seeds and trees with them. Indians took apple seeds and planted them in their villages, and John Chapman (later known as Johnny Appleseed) planted apple seeds wherever he went. Apples grow all over the United States, as well as around the world. Most apples are eaten raw, but they are also used for jellies, puddings, applesauce, dumplings, cider, juice, vinegar, and in many delicious baked foods. Some apples are dried and used for snacks. Have fun using apples in the following activities.

Applesauce

Provide an electric blender, cutting board, and knife and let children make their own snack. This recipe uses four peeled apples and yields two cups of sauce. Adjust the recipe to your class size.

Remind children to wash their hands before cooking! Wash the apples and cut each one into eighths. Pour a small amount of liquid (apple juice or water) into the blender and add four or five apple slices. Cover and process at PUREE until smooth. Change process to BLEND and add more apples, a few at a time.

Add $^1/_4$ cup sugar and $^1/_8$ tsp. cinnamon and blend in with the apples. **Tip:** If you're making a large quantity of applesauce, you can blend the apples and pour them into a large bowl until all of the apples have been processed. The sugar and cinnamon can be stirred into the processed apples in the bowl.

Apples for a Sweet New Year

At Rosh Hashanah, the Jewish people dip apple slices into honey and wish each other a sweet new year. You don't have to be Jewish to do this! Cut, core, and slice apples into small sections; then let each child dip a piece of apple into a bowl of honey. Before it is eaten, encourage them to wish each other a sweet year for learning.

Appealing Apple Recipes

Hot Apple Rings

Ingredients
1 c. biscuit mix
1 egg
1/2 c. milk
2 medium apples, peeled and cored

Use an electric mixer to beat the biscuit mix, egg, and milk until smooth. Grease an electric frying pan or stove top skillet with margarine. Cut the apples crosswise into 1/8" slices. Dip each slice into the batter; then cook in the pan until golden brown, turning once. Serve warm with jelly, syrup, or powdered sugar. This recipe makes about 2 dozen.

Apple Doughnuts

Ingredients

apples	raisins
peanut butter	small fruit chunks

Core several whole apples, then slice the apples so that each slice will have a center hole, creating an apple doughnut shape. Let children use craft sticks to spread peanut butter over their apple slices; then have them choose fruit chunks to set into the peanut butter and decorate their doughnuts.

Johnny Salad

Ingredients
6 c. pared, cubed apples
2 c. celery, sliced
1 c. seedless grapes
vanilla yogurt

Combine the apples, celery and grapes. Toss lightly. Stir in just enough vanilla yogurt to moisten the pieces.

Making Apple Chips

Weigh two apples on a scale, and record their weight. Cut the apples into thin slices and spread them on a plate. In three days, observe the apple slices. Note the changes. Weigh the slices and compare with their original weight. Why do they weigh less? Because the water in them has evaporated.

Apple Creatures for Halloween

Peel and core an apple, then cut a face into it. Push in two cloves for eyes. Mix together 1 part lemon juice, 1 part warm water, and 1 to 2 teaspoons of salt. Dip the whole apple into the mixture (this will help preserve it). Let it dry in a warm, dry place for a few days. Since the water in the apple evaporates, the apple will shrink and become wrinkled. The face will look like a witch or horrible creature. Extra features can be added by gluing on yarn hair, paper hats, and fabric scraps. Eyeglasses and antennae can be made from pipe cleaners.

Apple Science

Cut an apple in half, and cut each half into three pieces for a total of six pieces. Using your finger, a small brush, or cotton swab, cover the white sides of three apple pieces with lemon juice. Cover the sides of the other three apple pieces with water. Place all apple pieces on a paper towel and observe them every 15 minutes. What do your students observe happening? The pieces that were covered with water have turned brown, because the oxygen (air) has combined with other molecules. This is called oxidation. The pieces covered with lemon juice did not change color because the juice prevented the oxidation.

TRICKY TREATS FOR HALLOWEEN

Spiders

Ingredients

chocolate chips
chow mein noodles
miniature marshmallows
butterscotch chips
peanuts (optional)
cookie sheet/waxed paper

Melt chocolate and butterscotch chips in a double boiler on top of the stove. Add chow mein noodles (you may want to break them if they're too long). Add marshmallows and peanuts; stir until well covered. Drop on cookie sheet covered with waxed paper. Refrigerate until cool. Scrumpdelicious! Hint: Add ingredients slowly to melted chips making sure there is enough chocolate to cover.

Spooky Spider Salad

Ingredients

lettuce, shredded
tomato slices
green olives
cheese slices
corn

Sprinkle a shredded lettuce spiderweb on a plate. Set a tomato slice spider body on top of the lettuce. Top the tomato with olive slice eyes, a pimento nose, and a corn kernel mouth. Cut or tear the cheese slice into curvy strips. Place eight curved cheese strip legs around the tomato spider.

Count Dracula Drink

Combine 1 cup strawberries, 2 tablespoons honey, 4 cups milk, and a few drops of red food coloring in a blender. Cover tightly and blend until smooth.

Scarecrow Salad

Ingredients

peaches ($^1/_2$ peach each)
lettuce (1 whole leaf each)
celery sticks
raisins
pears ($^1/_2$ pear each)
carrot sticks
grapes
paper towels (2 each)

Have students wash lettuce and place one leaf on a double thick paper towel. Put one peach half on top of the lettuce; this is the scarecrow's head. Place one pear half just below the peach, small end up; this is the scarecrow's body. Using carrot and/or celery sticks, arrange them around the pear body for the scarecrow's arms and legs. Cut one big grape in half and place it below the celery/carrot legs for the scarecrow's feet. Place raisins at the end of the carrot/celery arms; these are the scarecrow's fingers. Eat and enjoy!

Ants on a Raft

Ingredients

raisins
Triscuits®/saltine crackers
cheese spread/peanut butter/cream cheese

Spread cream cheese, peanut butter or cheese spread over a square-shaped cracker. Place several raisins on top.

Ants on a Log

Ingredients

celery sticks
raisins
cheese spread/peanut butter/cream cheese

Wash celery; cut into 4" to 5" sticks. Spread cheese, peanut butter or cream cheese over celery stick. Place several raisins on top.

Owl Graham

Ingredients
whole graham crackers
raisins
peanut butter
walnut pieces
cheese slices
banana slices

Spread a circle of peanut butter on the bottom half of the graham cracker for the owl's chest. Add raisin "feathers" to the peanut butter. Cut a triangle from a cheese slice for the beak and place it above the chest. Above the beak, add two banana slice eyes. Dab peanut butter at the center of each banana slice; then set a raisin into the peanut butter. Dab peanut butter on the two upper corners of the graham cracker. Place a walnut piece "ear" in each corner.

Witches Hats

Ingredients
raisins
chocolate chips
sugar ice cream cones
bread slices
peanut butter

Have each child trim a bread slice into a circular shape. Spread peanut butter over the bread circle; then invert the ice cream cone onto the center of the bread slice to resemble a pointed witch hat. Spread peanut butter over the cone. Stick raisins and chocolate chips into the peanut butter as desired. It's a messy job, but somebody has to do it!

Jack-O'-Lantern Cookie Pops

Orange Icing

Ingredients

2 c. powdered sugar
2 T. butter, softened
2 T. margarine, softened
2 T. milk
1/2 tsp. orange flavoring
orange food coloring

Combine all of the above ingredients in a bowl. Beat with a mixer until light and fluffy.

Cookie Pops

Ingredients

oatmeal cookies
small pretzel sticks
orange icing
craft sticks
raisins

Place one oatmeal cookie on a plate or napkin, flat side up. Spread orange icing over the cookie. Break one pretzel stick in half and place both halves, side by side, into the icing at the top of the cookie, creating a stem. Place one end of a craft stick into the icing at the bottom of the cookie for a handle. Top with the flat side of the second oatmeal cookie. Spread icing over the second cookie and add raisin jack-o'-lantern features.

Cinnamon Toast Ghost

Ingredients

1/2 c. sugar
1/4 c. cinnamon
1/4 tsp. nutmeg
cream cheese
bread slices, toasted

Combine the sugar, cinnamon, and nutmeg in a small bowl. Pour it through a funnel into a recycled spice shaker. Tear the toasted bread into ghostly shapes. Spread cream cheese over the toast, then sprinkle with the cinnamon-sugar mixture.

Sweet November Treats

As Thanksgiving approaches, you and your children are sure to enjoy preparing these no-cook sweet treat recipes.

EDIBLE APPLE TURKEY

Insert toothpicks into an apple to create tail feathers. Have the children fill the toothpicks with goodies such as raisins, colored miniature marshmallows, chunks of cheese and so on. Draw a turkey head and cut it from cardboard. Have children color the facial features; then have the teacher make a small slit in the apple with a knife to insert the head inside.

Pilgrim's Pride

Ingredients
peach halves
cranberry sauce
orange slices
toothpicks

Set a peach half on a small plate, curved side down, for a boat. Fill the center of the peach half with cranberry sauce. Push a toothpick through an orange slice, then into the peach half to create a sail.

Natural Nutty Candy

Ingredients

3-4 cups dried fruit such as raisins, dates, figs, apricots, or mixed dried fruit bits
2 cups nuts such as almonds, walnuts, hazelnuts, or pecans
1 cup natural peanut butter

Chop 1 cup of nuts and set aside. Grind together remaining nuts and dried fruit. Mix peanut butter with fruit and nut mixture. Form into small balls. Roll balls in chopped nuts to cover. Store in refrigerator.

Natural candy provides a delicious and nutritious alternative to processed sweets. Children can invent combinations of fruits and nuts to mix together to create a variety of flavors.

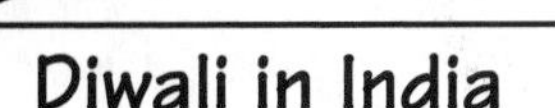

Diwali in India

Diwali is a festival celebrated in November by the people of India. It is one of the most beautiful holidays because in the evening people light oil lamps, and fireworks light up the sky. Celebrate Diwali by making kulfi, Indian ice cream.

Ingredients

1 cup evaporated milk
1 cup condensed milk
1 cup heavy cream
10 almonds
pinch of saffron
1 tsp. sugar

Blend all ingredients together. Freeze for four hours. Enjoy!

Tasty Tabletop Turkey

Materials

- potato
- kebob sticks
- toothpicks
- gumdrops
- marshmallow
- piece of licorice
- scissors

Directions

1. Firmly insert the ends of six toothpicks into the bottom of a potato, forming two side-by-side triangles. Turn the potato over. The toothpicks should provide a sturdy base for the turkey's feet.

2. Hold the potato with one hand and firmly insert three 5" kebob sticks across the top of the potato. Space sticks the length of the potato. Add four large gumdrops of various colors to each stick. Space gumdrops the length of each stick. The turkey now has feathers.

3. Insert the end of a toothpick into the middle front of the potato. Push a marshmallow onto the toothpick until it touches the potato. Then push the top of a 1" piece of licorice onto the toothpick until the licorice touches the marshmallow (licorice should hide the end of toothpick). The turkey now has a head and gobbler.

4. Cut pieces of gumdrop. Add these to the marshmallow to form the turkey's eyes and nose. Attach face with glue or toothpicks. The turkey is now complete. Place it on your table for a Thanksgiving centerpiece the whole family can enjoy.

Variations

Paint toothpicks and kebob sticks for colorful feathers and feet. Let sticks dry before inserting into potato. Raisins, m & m's®, and candy corn also make wonderful eyes and noses. Use your imagination on your turkey's face.

by Amanda Boor

Favorite Fall Recipes

As you find new recipes, cut and attach them to this page for future use.

Winter Warm-Ups

Welcome the season with some simple holiday treats.

Breakfast Soup

Ingredients
5 cups water
1 tsp. salt
2 cups oatmeal
3 ripe bananas
3/4 cup raisins
milk

Boil the water with the salt. Add the oatmeal and cook for five minutes. Mash the bananas and add them to the oatmeal. Stir in the raisins. Serve warm, adding milk if desired.

Cinnamon Stix

Ingredients
firm, dry bread slices
melted butter
1/4 cup confectioners' sugar
1 tsp. cinnamon
2 T. brown sugar
1/4 tsp. nutmeg

Mix the confectioners' sugar, brown sugar, cinnamon and nutmeg together. Set aside. Cut the firm, dry bread slices into strips. Dip the bread strips into the melted butter, then roll them in the spice mixture. Place the bread sticks on a cookie sheet and bake at 375°F for about 5 minutes, or until toasted.

Chicken Soup with Rice

A winter warm-up cooperative cooking craft that simply must be offered with a reading of the children's favorite, ***Chicken Soup with Rice*** *by Maurice Sendak.*

Materials

vegetable oil (approximately 3 tablespoons)
large onion slices
tablespoons of mild curry powder
cups of chicken stock
cups of diced celery
cups of diced carrots
cups of cooked, diced, skinless chicken
cups of cooked long grain rice
saltshaker
pepper shaker
¼ cup of dried parsley

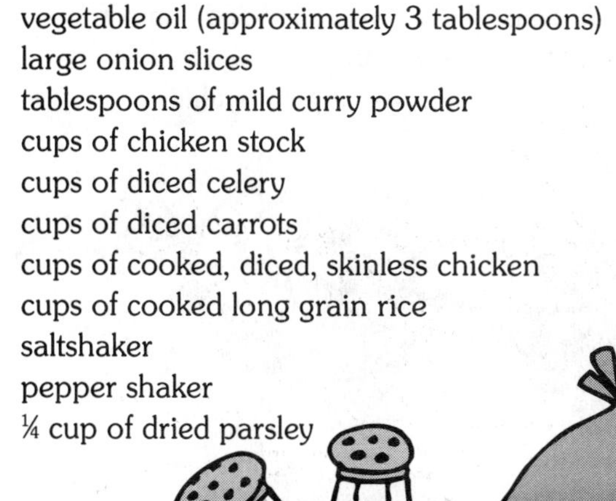

Let's Make It

1. Slice, dice, cook, and measure the ingredients into bowls.
2. Prepare a large recipe card or have children copy the recipe for individual use.
3. Have each child proceed down the assembly line, gathering the correct amount of each item into his or her bowl.
4. Have children pour their ingredients into the large cooking pot waiting at the end of the assembly line.
5. Bring to a boil, reduce heat, and simmer uncovered for 10 minutes. Stir in rice at this point; simmer for 1 minute.
6. Have an assistant fill each child's bowl either at the child's desk or on a tray that can be carried to desks.

Snow White Hot Chocolate

After playing in the snow or when celebrating a winter festival, there is nothing more satisfying than a steaming mug of hot chocolate. This recipe offers an aesthetically intriguing twist to an old favorite.

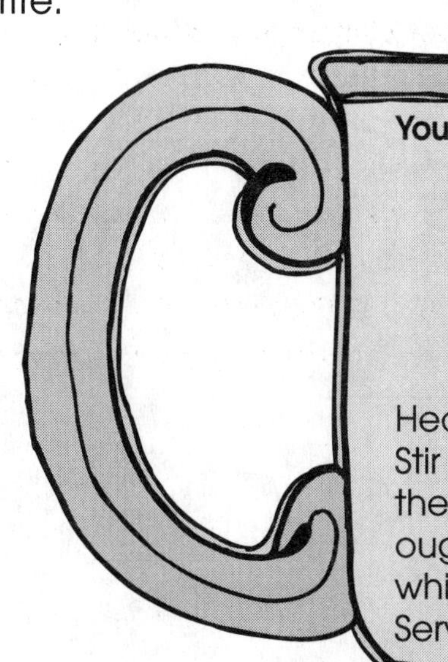

You Will Need

4 cups of water
12 cups of milk
large saucepan
wire whisk
mugs
(8 ounces) white chocolate baking squares
mini marshmallows, white chocolate shavings or whipped cream

Heat the white chocolate and the water over medium heat. Stir constantly until melted. Bring the mixture to a boil and then simmer for two minutes. Add the milk and heat thoroughly, stirring occasionally. Ladle into mugs, top with a fluffy white topping of marshmallows, shavings or whipped cream. Serves 25-30 children.

by Robynne Eagan

Season's Eatings

Lots of treat ideas that are easy classroom projects.

During the month of December, everyone is searching for new and different ideas. It is always an added bonus for the teacher to give a special treat to the class to enjoy while learning. It is also fun for children to make their own treats and share with other classes. Here are some holiday ideas that make creating and feasting enjoyable.

Be certain children know how these treats are constructed. The toothpicks should be removed prior to enjoying the treat.

by Jo Jo Cavalline and Jo Anne O'Donnell

Have a Pretzel Party

Make and bake pretzels. Then use them as decorations and snacks.

Pretzels

Ingredients

$^1/_2$ cup water
4 cups flour
1 egg mixed with 1 tablespoon of water
1 package dry yeast
1 tablespoon sugar
coarse salt

Mix water and yeast in a large bowl. Add 3 cups of flour and sugar to yeast mixture. Knead flour mixture by working in last cup of flour. Divide dough into enough pieces for class. Shape pretzels. Brush egg mixture on top of pretzel. Sprinkle with coarse salt. Bake 450°F for 25 minutes.

Let the children use their imaginations as they shape their pretzels or make into numerals for a math activity.

Christmas Punch 'n' Crunch

Santa Snack

English muffins
bread slices
cream cheese
strawberry jam
raisins
maraschino cherries
flaked coconut
red food coloring

Slice the muffins in half. Toast the muffin halves and bread slices. Tint softened cream cheese with red food coloring. Have children spread the tinted cream cheese over a muffin half for Santa's face and set it on a plate. Next, cut a triangle shape from a slice of toast, cover it with strawberry jam, and set it above the muffin for a hat. Add raisin eyes and a cherry nose to the muffin face. Sprinkle flaked coconut at the bottom of the face to create a beard and moustache. Add a raisin mouth in the center of this coconut. Sprinkle coconut over the jam to make a hatband and pom-pom.

Snow Grahams

Ingredients
graham crackers
marshmallow creme
flaked coconut

Break the graham crackers in half to form squares. Spoon marshmallow creme onto the graham crackers. Sprinkle the crackers with coconut "snow."

"Spice" Deer Cookies

Children love to cut shapes out of sugar cookie dough. Mix up your favorite sugar cookie recipe adding some cinnamon, ginger, and ground cloves. Roll out the dough and allow the children to cut cookies with reindeer-shaped cutters. Bake as directed and smell the spices.

Holiday Punch

You Will Need

20 ounces unsweetened frozen strawberries
46 ounces pineapple juice
lime sherbet

Puree the strawberries in a blender. Combine with the pineapple juice in a pitcher. Pour this punch into serving cups and garnish with a dollop of green lime sherbet.

Christmas Cookies

Make your favorite rolled sugar cookie mixture. Roll out the dough and cut out festive ornaments with cookie cutters. With a plastic drinking straw, make a hole at the top of each cookie. Bake as directed. Now the kids can frost and decorate the cookies. Place ribbon or yarn through the hole to hang the "cookie ornaments" on your classroom tree.

Crunch Christmas Trees

You Will Need

1/4 cup margarine
1-10 oz. package (40 large) or 4 cups miniature marshmallows
green food coloring
6 cups crispy rice cereal
decorations such as cinnamon red hots, silver ball candy sprinkles

In a large saucepan, melt the margarine over low heat. Add the marshmallows and stir until melted. Add drops of food coloring until you reach the desired shade. Remove from the heat.

Add the cereal to the marshmallow mixture. Stir well. To make tree shapes, lightly grease a 1-cup funnel. Pack it with the cereal mixture. When full, turn it upside down and unmold it on a plate. While it's still warm, press in the candies.

Note: This recipe makes five trees. Increase the ingredients according to your class size.

Christmas Cupcakes

Prepare cupcake batter according to package directions. Fold in chopped red and green maraschino cherries. Bake as directed. Use canned vanilla frosting, and make it festive by adding food coloring.

Santa's Trail Mix

Package three to four cups of Santa's Trail Mix in brown lunch bags. Fold the top down twice. Punch two holes in the center of the folds. Slip a length of twine through the holes and tie in a bow. Attach the poem and you have great gifts straight from the kitchen of Mrs. Claus! This recipe makes about 10 to 12 bags.

Santa's Trail Mix is lots of fun to make and even more fun to give. Have students give Santa's Trail Mix as a special holiday treat to school secretaries, principal, nurse, janitors and other school friends.

Santa's Trail Mix also makes a fun, inexpensive gift for your students. Just follow the simple recipe Mrs. Claus has passed down from generation to generation. Allow the students' imaginations to fly by having them make up and share stories about how the trail mix saved Santa, the elves and the reindeer from various dangers during their Christmas Eve ride.

by Jo Jo Cavalline and Jo Anne O'Donnell

Santa's Trail Mix

Ingredients

2 cups salted peanuts
5 cups Cheerios® cereal
5 cups Wheat Chex®
10 oz. mini pretzels
2 packages vanilla chips
1 lb. M & M's®
3 T. cooking oil

very large bowl or pan
microwave oven
microwave-safe bowl
spoon for stirring
measuring cups and spoons
waxed paper

Mix all the ingredients (except the vanilla chips and oil) in the large bowl or pan. Melt the vanilla chips and oil in the microwave until creamy. Pour the creamy vanilla mixture over the dry ingredients. Stir until all of the dry mix is coated. Spread the coated trail mix on waxed paper to dry. (This only takes about 30 minutes.)

Santa's Trail Mix

This special Christmas trail mix is made each year
for Santa, the elves and all the reindeer.
They have a nibble in each hemisphere
On their annual trip to spread Christmas cheer.

Rudolph

The Tasty Reindeer

Materials

- paper napkin
- scissors
- red apple
- thin pretzel sticks
- raisins
- nuts or a cracker

Directions

1. Fold a square napkin into a triangle shape. Then fold the top two corners down to make Rudolph's ears.
2. Cut two slits on the folded side of Rudolph's head.
3. Place pretzel sticks in the slits to make Rudolph's antlers.
4. Place raisins on the napkin for Rudolph's eyes.
5. Polish a red apple till it's shiny. Ask an adult to cut off a round slice of the apple. Place the slice on the bottom corner of the napkin to be Rudolph's shiny red nose.
6. Eat Rudolph (except for the napkin, of course). Make more Rudolphs, or make Rudolph's reindeer friends with a few nuts or a small cracker for their brown noses.

Reindeer Sandwiches

This fancy sandwich is sure to put smiles on the children's faces. They can even help in the preparation. You will need whole wheat bread, peanut butter, jelly, pretzel sticks, sliced carrot rounds, and small red gumdrops. Cut a slice of bread into two triangles. Fill triangles with peanut butter and jelly. Insert six pretzel sticks (three on each side) to the top of the sandwich for antlers. Put on carrot eyes and a red gumdrop nose at the tip.

Christmas Bells

Ingredients

lettuce, shredded
pear halves
flaked coconut
red food coloring
pretzel sticks
maraschino cherries

Sprinkle shredded lettuce on a plate. Top with the pear half, flat side down. Tint the coconut with red food coloring, and sprinkle it over the pear half. Push a pretzel stick into the narrow end of the pear half for a handle, and set a cherry clapper below the wide end.

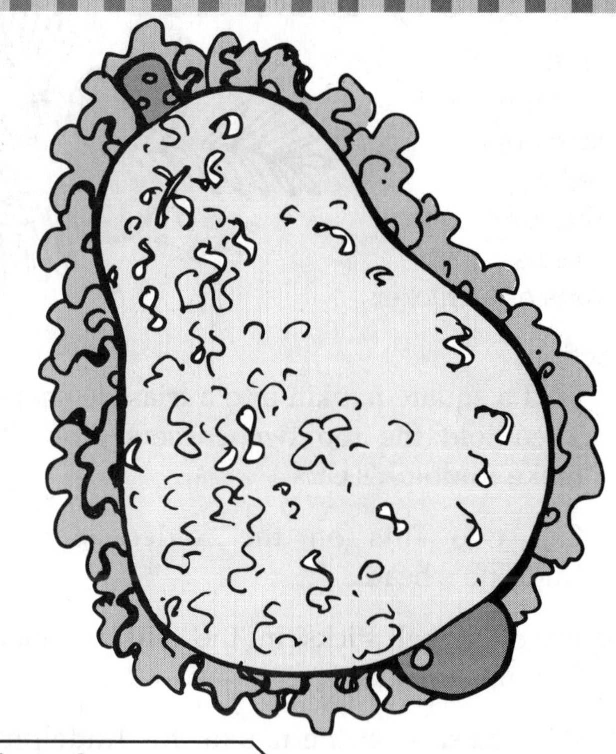

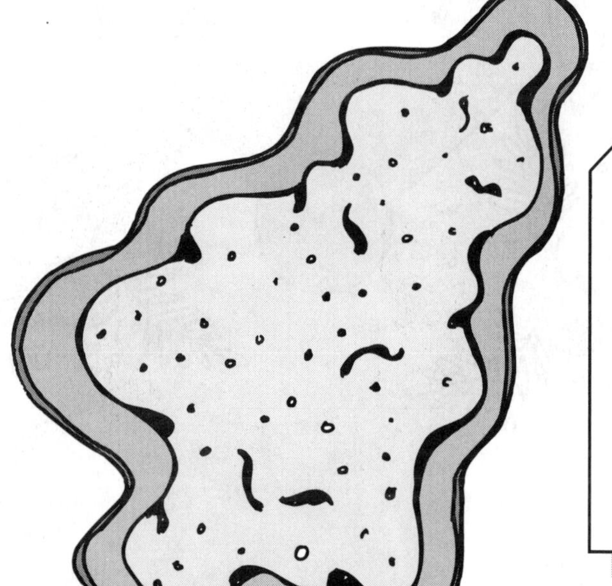

Tree Treats

Ingredients

bread slices
cream cheese
red and green food coloring
granulated sugar

Toast the bread slices. Using a cookie cutter, cut tree shapes from the toast. Tint the cream cheese with the green food coloring and spread onto trees. Tint the sugar with the red food coloring and sprinkle over the cream cheese.

Candle Salad

Ingredients

shredded lettuce
pineapple slices
bananas
cherries
toothpicks

Place shredded lettuce on plate. Lay a pineapple slice on the lettuce. Cut the banana in half vertically and stand one half up, on top of the pineapple slice, over the hole. Attach a cherry to the top of the banana candle with a toothpick.

by Marie E. Cecchini

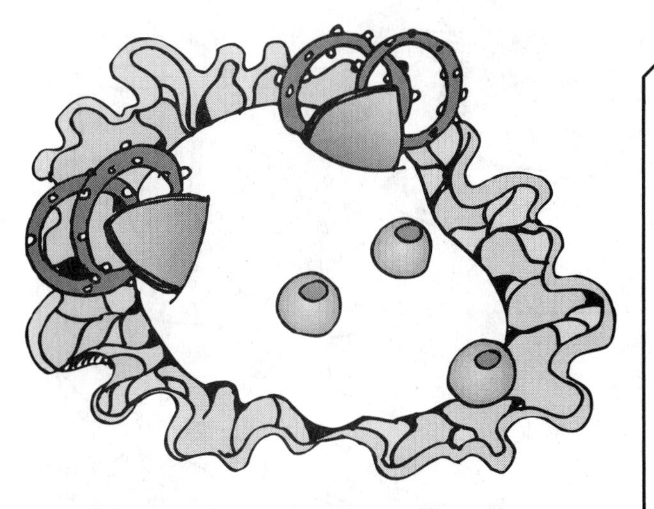

Rudolph Salad

Ingredients

lettuce leaf
pear half
almond slices
cherries
cranberries, halved
"3-ring" pretzels

Set the lettuce leaf on a plate. Lay the pear half on the lettuce leaf, flat side down. Add the cherry to the narrow end of the pear, for a nose. Use two cranberry halves for eyes. Push two almond slices into the pear near the back for ears. Push pretzels into the pear behind the ears for antlers.

Christmas Mouse

Ingredients

lettuce leaf
hard-boiled egg
peanuts
cinnamon candies
licorice string
cheese, shredded
whole cloves (for decorative purposes only)

Set the lettuce leaf on a plate. Slice the egg lengthwise and set it on the lettuce, flat side down. Push two peanut halves into the egg near the narrow end for mouse ears. Push two cloves into the egg for eyes. Push a cinnamon candy into the front for a nose. Set a piece of licorice string at the back for a tail. Sprinkle shredded cheese onto the plate around the mouse.

Blizzard Frosty

Ingredients

milk
softened ice cream
instant pudding
small jars or cups with lids

Have each child measure 1 c. milk, 2 Tbls. instant pudding and 1 scoop of ice cream into a container. Seal the containers tightly; then create a "blizzard" by shaking the mixture for at least one minute before drinking. **Variation:** Combine all of the ingredients in a blender, mix well, and pour into glasses.

Either/Or Cookies

Ingredients

1/2 cup butter/margarine
3 cups oatmeal
1 cup honey
3 T. cocoa powder
3/4 cup powdered milk
1/2 tsp. salt
2 tsp. vanilla
1/2 cup peanut butter
1/2 cup raisins

Melt the butter in a saucepan over low heat. Add the oatmeal and stir well. Add the honey, cocoa powder, powdered milk, salt, vanilla, peanut butter and raisins. Use your hands to mix well. Batter will be stiff. Bake at 350°F, or refrigerate for about an hour, then eat.

Note: This batter also makes excellent molding material. However, be sure to flour both working surface and hands before creating any holiday shapes, as the dough is quite sticky.

Snow Toasties

Ingredients

bread slices
red jelly (strawberry or raspberry)
confectioners' sugar
holiday cookie cutters

Toast the bread slices. Use the cookie cutters to cut the toasted bread into holiday shapes. Place a spoonful of jelly on top of each shape; then sprinkle with confectioners' sugar to look like snow.

Gumdrop Pops

Ingredients

gumdrop candies
milk
confectioners' sugar
toothpicks

Stick a toothpick into each gumdrop. Dip the gumdrops into milk, then sprinkle them with confectioners' sugar. Eat them as mini lollipops, or add a few to the top of a party cupcake.

Snowy-Day Salad

Ingredients

lettuce leaves
pear halves
cottage cheese
raisins
cinnamon red-hot candies
black olives

Lay a lettuce leaf on a plate. Top with a pear half, flat side down. Cover the pear half with cottage cheese to resemble snow. Use raisins to give the snowperson eyes, buttons and a mouth. Add a cinnamon candy nose. For a top hat, slice a black olive in half, and arrange the halves perpendicular to each other above the head.

Edible Angel

Ingredients

bread slices
cheese slices
cream cheese
pretzel rings
golden raisins
cucumber slices

Toast the bread slices and cut into triangles. Top one triangle with a cheese triangle and set on a plate for the body. Spread cream cheese over two additional triangles and set at the top point of the body for wings. Place a cucumber slice above the wings for a head. Add a pretzel ring above the head as a halo. Set raisin feet below the cheese body.

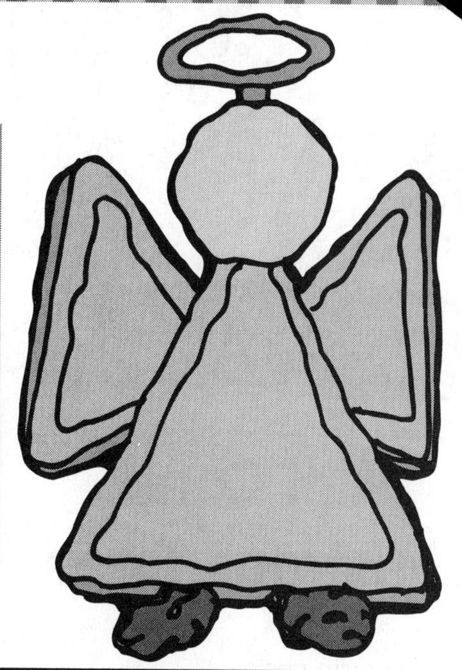

Bagel Wreath

Ingredients

mini bagels
flaked coconut
maraschino cherries
whipped cream cheese
raisins
green food coloring

Slice bagels in half and tint coconut with green food coloring. Have the children spread cream cheese over bagels; then sprinkle green coconut over the cream cheese. Let them add raisin and cherry decorations to their wreaths.

Snowball Sundae

Ingredients

vanilla ice cream
flaked coconut
maraschino cherries

Help the children place one scoop of ice cream on a plate or in a cup. Let them sprinkle coconut "snow" over the ice cream; then top it with a cherry.

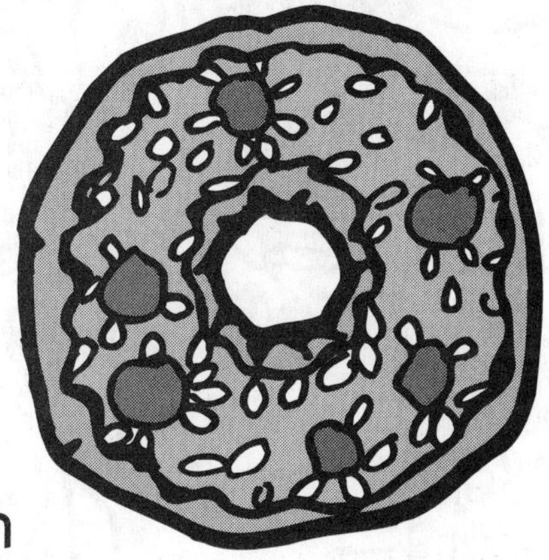

Snack'n On

Have each child bring in one white food item for snack (popcorn, marshmallows, milk, ice cream, turnips, bananas, apples, cream cheese, string cheese, and so on). Spread out a white tablecloth with white napkins and paper plates for a wintertime picnic. Don't forget the raisin "ants!"

Mini Cone Christmas Trees

Materials

royal icing (See recipe below.)
mini cones (for ice cream)
pastry bags and decorating tips
craft sticks
cookie decorations: colored sprinkles, silver balls, small candies

Recipe for Royal Icing

3 egg whites
1/2 tsp. (2 ml) cream of tartar
pinch of salt
1 lb. (500 g) confectioner's sugar

1. Beat the egg whites, cream of tartar, and salt until soft peaks form.
2. Cover the mixture with a damp cloth until needed.

Let's Make It

1. Have children dip the bottom of the cone in the icing, and then place upside down on a doily on a square or circle of cardboard.
2. Children can coat the cone with icing, and then sprinkle and press decorations on the Christmas tree while icing is still damp. Cover with a damp cloth if necessary to dampen.
3. Colored or white frosting may be squeezed over the creation using the pastry bag and tip. Let dry.
4. Place the festive trees around the classroom for decorations, or have children take them home.
5. Children can eat these creations when they have finished admiring them.

Christmas Yule Log

16 large marshmallows
1 cup crunchy peanut butter
3 tablespoons butter or margarine
2 tablespoons milk
1 teaspoon vanilla
1 cup raisins or flaked coconut
1 cup uncooked quick oatmeal
1 cup crushed peanuts

Melt marshmallows, peanut butter, and butter or margarine over very low heat or hot water. Add milk and vanilla and mix well. Then stir the uncooked oatmeal and raisins or coconut into the mixture. It will be very stiff. Place on waxed paper or a cookie sheet. Form into two or three "logs" and roll them in the crushed peanuts. Place them in the refrigerator. If pieces are too big, cut carefully to size.

Honey Gingerbread Cookies

Ingredients

3 cups sifted flour
1/2 cup sugar
1 teaspoon salt
2 teaspoons baking soda
1/2 lb. butter or margarine cut into bits
2 teaspoons cinnamon
1/2 teaspoon powdered cloves
1/2 teaspoon powdered nutmeg
2 teaspoons powdered ginger
1/2 cup honey

Sift dry ingredients—flour, sugar, baking soda, salt, ginger, cinnamon, cloves, and nutmeg—together into a mixing bowl. With fingertips, blend bits of butter into dry ingredient mixture. When butter has been thoroughly mixed in, add the honey. Stir until blended. Refrigerate for one to two hours. Roll dough about 1/8" thick between sheets of waxed paper or onto a floured cutting board. Use cookie cutters in shapes of gingerbread men or houses. Preheat oven to 350°F. Bake for 12 to 15 minutes on a cookie sheet. Remove from oven and allow cookies to cool one minute before removing with a spatula to cool on wire cake racks. Decorate with red, green, and white holiday frosting if you wish.

Invite some mothers to assist with this baking treat.

Delicious Decorations

Have fun making these decorations for your classroom.
Then kids can delight in eating these edible ornaments.

Christmas Wreaths

Materials: large box of crispy rice cereal, vanilla, green food coloring, margarine, bag of large marshmallows, butter, waxed paper, red cinnamon candies

Melt together 1/2 cup of margarine, 30 marshmallows and 1 teaspoon of vanilla in a saucepan. When mixture is creamy, add food coloring. Remove from heat and stir in cereal to make a firm mixture, mixing well.

When the mixture has cooled to the touch, let children butter their fingers and form the cereal into the shape of wreaths. Use the cinnamon candies as berries.

Let the wreaths harden on waxed paper, then tie on a ribbon and hang up.

Cookie Handprints

Materials: your favorite sugar cookie recipe or commercial refrigerated cookie dough, candy decorations like sprinkles, ribbon

Roll out dough to 1/2" thickness on floured waxed paper. Have each child lay his/her hand on the dough and carefully cut out the hand shape. Let children decorate, making sure they poke a hole at the wrist end of the cookie for hanging. Carefully transfer the handprint to a baking sheet and bake according to recipe directions.

Variation: Painted Cookie Handprints: Mix 1 egg yolk with 1/4 teaspoon of water. Divide the mixture into several small cups. Add a different color of food coloring to each cup. (If paint thickens, add a few drops of water.) Use a paintbrush to paint designs on each cookie.

Gingerbread Men Garland

Materials: one package of gingerbread mix, flour, gingerbread man cutter, raisins, red cinnamon candies

Mix gingerbread mix with 1/4 cup warm water. Knead dough on floured surface until smooth. Roll dough to 1/8" thickness and cut out "men" with cutter.

Place "men" on greased baking sheet and decorate with raisins and candies. Be sure to poke a hole in the top of each "man" for hanging. Bake 6 to 8 minutes in 375° oven.

When cool, use ornament hanger or paper clips to hang "men" from a length of pretty ribbon.

Easy Stringing Garland

Materials: 1/4" wide or smaller ribbon, cereal with holes (such as Froot Loops™), LifeSavers™, pretzels, popcorn, cranberries, blunt-ended needles

Young children can work entirely with cereal and pretzels; older children will enjoy using the needles to thread popcorn and cranberries, as well as candies and other goodies.

Hanukkah Delights

The eight-day December Hanukkah celebration changes dates from year to year. But every year potato pancakes (latkes) remain Hanukkah favorites.

Menorah Crackers

Ingredients

graham crackers
bananas
peanut butter
raisins

Have the children spread peanut butter over whole graham crackers. Cut the bananas into sticks for candles. Have the children place nine banana stick candles onto the peanut butter. Set a raisin flame above each banana candle.

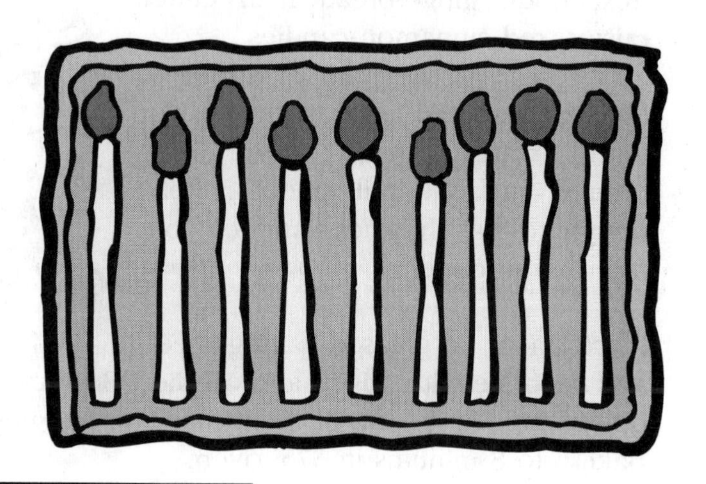

Dreidel Snack

Ingredients

bread slices
soft cream cheese
raisins
carrot sticks
blue food coloring

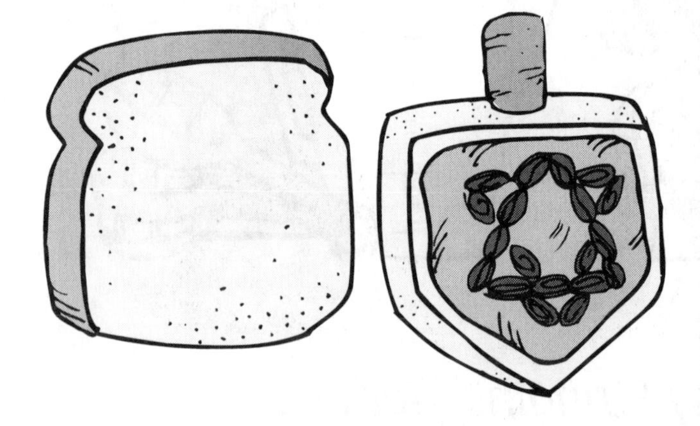

Toast the bread slices and tint the cream cheese with the food coloring. Have the children cut off two corners of their toast slices to form the shape of a dreidel. Spread blue cream cheese over the dreidel-shaped toast. Use raisins to make one of the symbols used on dreidels in the cream cheese. Set a carrot stick handle at the top of the dreidel. Note: Display dreidels or pictures of dreidels so children can copy the symbols onto their snacks.

Potato Pancakes

Ingredients

2 c. grated potatoes
1 sm. onion, grated
vegetable oil
pinch salt and pepper
1/2 c. bread crumbs or matzoh meal
2 eggs
pinch baking powder
applesauce

Mix all ingredients together except for oil and applesauce. Heat frying pan with a little oil in bottom of pan. When hot, spoon mixture into frying pan and make small pancakes. When golden brown on one side, turn and cook other side. Drain and eat with applesauce.

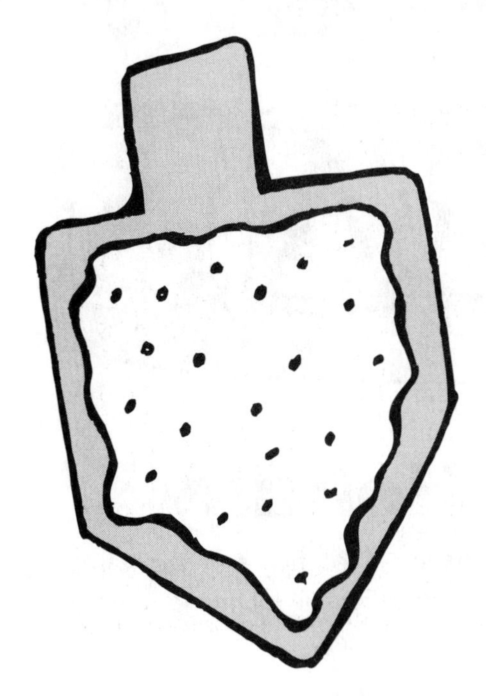

Dreidel Toast

Ingredients

bread slices
cream cheese
blue and yellow food coloring
granulated sugar

Toast the bread slices. Cut the top and bottom of each slice to a point, leaving the sides straight, so the toast resembles a dreidel. Tint the cream cheese with blue food coloring and spread it over the toast. Tint the sugar with the yellow food coloring and sprinkle over the cream cheese.

Delicious Dreidel

You Will Need

1 marshmallow
1 toothpick
1 Hershey's Kiss® (candy)

Poke the toothpick through the marshmallow. Add the Kiss to the end to form a spinning top—a dreidel to spin and to eat, too!

Star of David Sandwich

Ingredients

bread slices
hard-boiled eggs
mayonnaise
grated cheddar cheese

Peel and chop the eggs. Combine the eggs with a small amount of mayonnaise and set aside. Toast the bread slices and cut them into triangles. Spread egg mixture over two triangles. Set one egg triangle over the other, egg sides up, to form a six-pointed star. Sprinkle cheddar cheese over the star.

An African American Holiday

Kwanzaa is a nonreligious holiday honoring African American people and their past. Dr. Maulana Karenga, an African American teacher, first celebrated Kwanzaa in 1966. For seven days (December 26 until January 1), people learn more about the customs and history of Africa.

The term Kwanzaa means "first fruits of the harvest." This word comes from the Swahili language and represents all ethnic groups of Africa.

This holiday is for family and friends to spend time together and create their own customs. This celebration encourages learning more about Africa and the history of African Americans.

Food for Kwanzaa Celebrations

During Kwanzaa, help your students prepare African food in the classroom. Use the traditional foods of Africa to make a fruit salad for your Kwanzaa celebration.

- 2 lemons
- 2 bananas
- 1/2 pound seedless grapes
- 1 cup nuts
- 2 cups cantaloupe or melon, cubed
- water
- 2 apples
- 4 kiwi
- 2 oranges, sectioned
- 1/2 cup coconut
- 1/2 cup sugar

Cut the lemons in half. Squeeze the juice into a bowl. Set aside. Slice or cut the fruit in cubes. Combine in a large bowl. Sprinkle with the lemon juice.

Make a syrup of 2 cups water and 1/2 cup sugar. Bring to a boil and cook for two minutes. Allow to cool and pour over fruit. Add coconut and nuts. Refrigerate until ready to serve.

by Carolyn Ross Tomlin

Kwanzaa Fruit Shapes

Ingredients

4 4oz. pkgs. fruit-flavored gelatin
2 1/2 c. boiling water
fruit chunks and slices

Combine gelatin and boiling water in a mixing bowl. Stir to completely dissolve gelatin, then pour into a 9" x 13" oblong baking dish. Allow gelatin to stand for about 30 minutes, until it begins to thicken. Then place fruit chunks and slices throughout pan. Refrigerate until firm, then cut into shapes with cookie cutters.

Nutty Bananas

Two favorite African foods are bananas and peanuts. Make this fun snack in your classroom.

Place a craft stick in each banana and freeze on a tray lined with waxed paper. Melt chocolate morsels in a pot. Dip the banana into the chocolate sauce, and then roll it on a plate of finely chopped peanuts. What a yummy treat!

Sweet Potato Pie

Ingredients

2 c. sweet potatoes, drained
3 eggs
1 tsp. cinnamon
3/4 c. milk
1 9" pie shell, baked
4 T. margarine, melted
1 c. sugar
1/4 tsp. grated nutmeg
1 tsp. vanilla
1/4 c. chopped pecans

Use a food processor or fork to mash sweet potatoes with melted margarine. Blend in eggs, sugar, cinnamon and nutmeg. Add milk and vanilla. Pour mixture into baked pie shell. Microwave on 70% (medium high) 7 minutes. Sprinkle pecans over surface of pie. Rotating midway through cooking; microwave on 70% (medium high) 6 to 8 minutes or until center no longer jiggles. If you prefer, you can bake it in the oven at 375°F for about 35-45 minutes or until it doesn't jiggle.

St. Lucia's Day

Celebrating Christmas in Sweden

In Sweden, Christmas celebrations start on December 13th, which is St. Lucia's Day. On the morning of this day, young girls in each family dress to represent St. Lucia, Queen of Light. She dresses in a long white robe, red sash and wears an evergreen wreath on her head adorned with candles. Sweden has long winter nights, so St. Lucia's candles represent the taking away of darkness. She serves a breakfast of saffron buns and coffee to her parents. If there are other girls in the family, they dress up also. Brothers are called star boys, wearing long white shirts and a cone-shaped hat decorated with stars.

From this day until Christmas, the homemakers and mothers are busy cooking special foods for this holiday. One of these dishes is called *lutfisk* made from fine fish of the season. Rice porridge *(risgrynsgrot)* has a special almond hidden inside. Whoever finds it is promised good fortune.

Prepare two traditional Swedish Christmas treats: holiday bread called Julekaka and Lussekatter.

Julekaka

1 loaf frozen bread dough (thawed)
1/2 cup candied fruit including raisins
1/4 teaspoon cardamom
1/4 teaspoon cinnamon

Roll out the dough in a big circle about 1/2" thick. Sprinkle on the spices and candied fruit. Roll up the dough and shape into a long roll. Place this on a greased cookie sheet. Let the dough rest and rise in a warm place for at least one hour. Bake the bread at 350°F for 30-40 minutes. Remove the bread and let it cool on a rack.

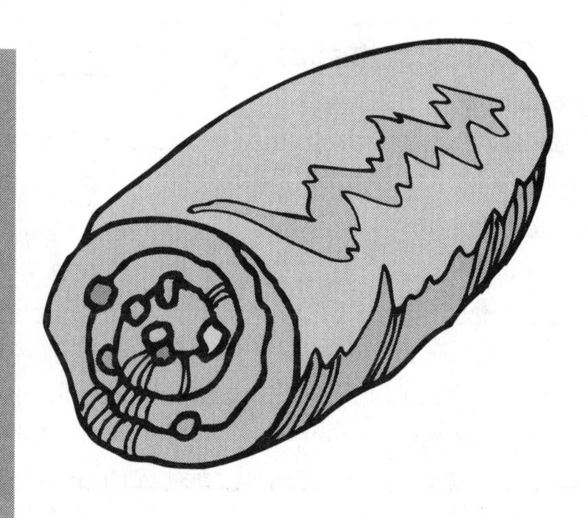

Lussekatter

Ingredients

package of refrigerated biscuits
powdered sugar glaze
raisins

Give each student one biscuit. Roll the biscuit into a rope about 8" long. Form the dough into an X. Decorate with raisins. Bake according to package directions. Brush with a glaze made from the powdered sugar and water. Serve warm.

Sinterklaas

Celebrating Christmas in Holland

A special part of the Dutch feast Sinterklaas is a pastry called Letterblankets. These edible letters are a flaky puff pastry filled with almond paste. Letterblankets are put at each individual guest's place at the feasting table. A giant *M* might be in the mother's place or might even be used as the centerpiece. Each guest's first name initial marks their special place at the table. Following is a recipe you and family members can make for your Christmas table.

Letterblankets

1 cup almond paste
1/4 cup granulated sugar
1 large egg
pastry for two 9" pie crusts
1 egg lightly beaten with 1 tablespoon milk

Heat oven to 375° F. In a small bowl, stir almond paste, sugar and egg. Chill while rolling pastry. Roll out half of the pastry about 1/4" thick into a square. Cut into 2" wide strips. On lightly greased baking sheet, lay strips to form letter *M* approximately 10" high and 10" wide. Press marzipan on top of letter, leaving a 1/2" border on all sides. Roll remaining pastry in similar fashion. Brush border of *M* with egg glaze, and place second layer of strips over marzipan. Press edges together. Brush surface with egg glaze. Bake 35 minutes until evenly browned.

Legend of Old Befana

Celebrating Christmas in Italy

In a small village in Italy, there was an old woman who spent her days sweeping her little house and walks. She also liked to bake cookies. One day she heard noises and saw a procession of royal-looking men, camels and horses crossing her path. They said they were looking for the way to Bethlehem to find the Child King. Old Befana decided she would bake cookies to take to the child and also try to find Him. She searched and searched, but with no success. The legend says that every year on January 6 (The Feast of the Three Kings), Old Befana visits all the children of Italy and leaves them candies, cookies and gifts. It is said that she is still searching for the Christ Child.

The Legend of Old Befana

by Tomie dePaola, HBJ Publishing, 1980

Sugar Cookies

This is a good story to read and then bake cookies together afterward. There are many recipes for sugar cookies, and even easy refrigerator dough for convenience. Here is a standard sugar cookie recipe.

1 c. softened butter
3/4 c. sugar
1 large egg
1 tsp. vanilla extract
2 3/4 c. flour
1 tsp. baking soda
1 tsp. cream of tartar

Cream the butter and sugar in a large bowl until fluffy. Add the egg and vanilla and beat well. Combine the flour, baking soda and cream of tartar in a container and slowly add it to the butter mixture until thoroughly combined. Refrigerate the dough until cool. Then work it with your hands until pliable. Place it on a floured board and roll out the dough until it is 1/4" thick. Cut the dough with cookie cutters. Bake these cookies in a preheated 350°F oven for 8 to 10 minutes. You can spread sugar on the dough before baking or spread them with frosting and sugar when they are baked and cooled.

Celebrate Soup and Pancakes

Celebrate National Soup Month in January with a tasty new recipe.
Then celebrate National Pancake Month in February and prepare pancake bears.

Snowperson Soup

Ingredients

applesauce
vanilla yogurt
raisins
orange marmalade or tangerine slices

Have each child measure 1/2 cup of applesauce and 1/2 cup vanilla yogurt into a small bowl, then stir to combine. Let them use the backs of their spoons to smooth the mixture and cover the bottoms of their bowls. Place raisins over the mixture for eyes and a mouth. Add a spoonful of marmalade or an orange or tangerine slice mouth.

Pancake Bears

Ingredients

"complete" pancake mix
water
syrup or jam
raisins

Prepare pancakes as directed on package, in small, medium, and large sizes. Have children place one large pancake on a plate for the bear's body, and a medium one above it for a head. Let them place small pancakes in appropriate places for arms, legs, and ears. Have children cover the pancakes with syrup or spread them with jam, then add raisin facial features.

A Variety of Valentine Treats

Happy Hearts

Ingredients:

1 cup butter
1 egg
1 tsp. vanilla extract
$1\frac{1}{2}$ tsp. baking powder
vanilla frosting
red shoestring licorice
heart-shaped cookie cutter
1 cup sugar
3 T. milk
3 cups flour
$\frac{1}{2}$ tsp. salt
cinnamon hearts
icing tube

Cream butter and sugar together in medium-size mixing bowl. Beat in egg, vanilla and milk. Stir in flour, baking powder and salt until well mixed. Preheat oven to 400°F. Roll out dough, $\frac{1}{3}$ at a time, on a floured surface to $\frac{1}{8}$" thickness. Using cookie cutter, cut into heart shapes. Place 1" apart on ungreased baking sheets. Bake for 5-8 minutes (until golden brown).

Once cookies have cooled, fill icing tube with frosting and have children outline the inside of their cookie heart. Have them put a small squirt of icing where the eyes, nose and mouth would go. Place a cinnamon heart on the two spots for the eyes and for the nose. Cut 1" pieces of licorice and put on the frosting spots for the mouth and eyebrows. Have a heart and enjoy!

Crackers with Heart

Ingredients:

snack crackers
red food coloring
cinnamon hearts
frosting (or cream cheese)
large marshmallows
tongue depressor sticks

Give each student a snack cracker. Add a couple drops of red food coloring to the frosting or cream cheese; stir until blended. Have the students use a stick to spread some frosting or cream cheese over their cracker. Place a big marshmallow on top of the frosting. Add a little more frosting to the top of the marshmallow. Stick a cinnamon heart on top.

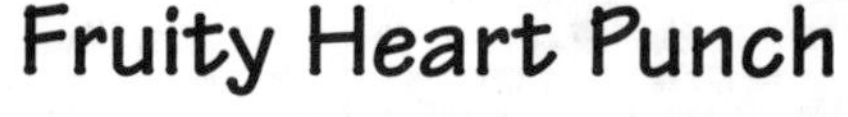

Fruity Heart Punch

Mix one large can of unsweetened pineapple juice, six cups of water and one package of tropical fruit punch soft drink mix. Stir well. Prior to the party, freeze maraschino cherries into each section of several ice cube trays. Place a "cherried" ice cube into a clear cup and add this delicious punch.

Candy Bar Wrapper Valentines

Save candy bar wrappers for this project. Children cut large paper hearts and combine a few written words with words cut from the candy bar wrappers to create a valentine message. For example, "Valentine, you send me to Mars" (using a Mars® bar wrapper), or "Valentine, for you I would travel the Milky Way" (using a Milky Way® wrapper) or "Hugs and Kisses" (using Hershey's Kisses® wrappers).

Valentine Heart Animals

Children trace hearts of all sizes and colors, not just the traditional red, pink, and white hearts. The hearts are cut out and put together to create animals. Use the scraps to make ears, faces, and tails. Children write valentine messages on the animals and present them to friends and family.

Jelly Heart Sandwiches

Make sandwiches with strawberry jelly. Place a heart-shaped cookie cutter in the center of the sandwich and press firmly to make heart-shaped sandwiches. Munch on the scraps and set the sandwiches aside until everyone has had a turn. Serve the jelly heart sandwiches with pink strawberry-flavored milk or red fruit punch.

Something for the Birds

A sweet and sticky project, this is something children will enjoy making for winter birds. If your classroom looks out over an area with trees, hang a completed pinecone bird feeder where children can observe birds using the feeder. Children will also enjoy taking a feeder home to enjoy with their families.

Offer the birds a treat on a cold winter day.

Materials

water table
plastic bins
birdseed
peanut butter or suet
pinecones
wooden craft sticks
lengths of yarn or string
small plastic tubs with lids or plastic bags that seal
labels and pencils
hand-washing facilities

Let's Make It

1. Fill one bin with birdseed and another with suet or peanut butter.
2. Place the bins, string, and craft sticks inside your empty water table. This will help to contain the mess!
3. Have students begin by tying a string to a pinecone.
4. Once the string is securely fastened, children can use the craft stick to cover their pinecone with peanut butter or suet.
5. The gooey pinecone can then be rolled and squashed into the birdseed.
6. Place the completed pinecone in a plastic tub or bag that can be sealed. Label each package.
7. Children can take the pinecone bird feeder home and hang it in a place where they can watch the birds feast.

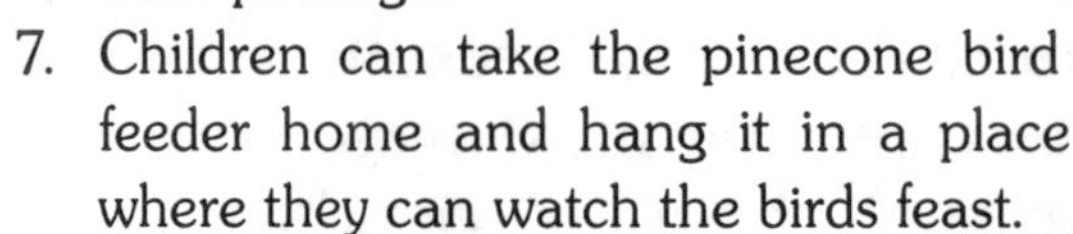

Favorite Winter Recipes

As you find new recipes, cut and attach them to this page for future use.

Popular Peanut Butter

March is Peanut Month and March 1st is Peanut Butter Lovers' Day. Celebrate the popular peanut with these tasty treats.

Peanut Butter Fondue

Ingredients

1 c. creamy peanut butter
1 c. light cream
1/2 c. honey
fruit chunks—apples, peaches, pears, bananas, etc.

Measure peanut butter into a fondue pot or saucepan. Blend in the cream and honey. Heat over low heat, stirring constantly until the mixture starts to boil. Reduce heat to warm. Have children prepare the fruit. Have children spear fruit with forks and dip into mixture.

Crunchy Peanut Treats

Ingredients

1/2 c. peanut butter
1/2 c. peanuts
3 c. chow mein noodles
1 c. butterscotch or chocolate pieces

Stir and melt candy pieces with peanut butter over a double boiler until smooth. Remove the mixture from heat and stir in peanuts and chow mein noodles. Mix well to coat. Drop by spoonfuls onto waxed paper and refrigerate until set, about 30 minutes.

Superhero Celery Sticks

Ingredients

celery
toothpicks
raisins
lettuce leaves
carrot slices
peanut butter

Fill a stalk of celery with peanut butter. Using the wide end of the celery as the top, place two raisins in the peanut butter for eyes; then add a raisin nose. Cut a carrot slice in half and set in the peanut butter as the mouth. Wrap a lettuce leaf cape around the celery stalk just below the mouth and secure it with a toothpick. Remind the children to remove the toothpick before eating.

Lunch and Crunch

Quick and easy recipes for nutritious lunches or recess crunches!

Tic-Tac-Toe Lunch

Ingredients

white bread
sandwich spread
(peanut butter, egg or tuna salad)
wheat bread
cheese slices

Cut the bread slices into squares. Use these squares with your choice of spread to make mini sandwiches. Arrange the sandwiches on a tray in three rows of three, alternating bread colors. The layout should resemble a checkerboard. Cut the cheese slices into circles (for Os) and strips (for Xs) and place the Os and Xs on top of the sandwiches.

Crunchy Raisin Salad

Ingredients

2 lbs. carrots, shredded
$3/4$ cup celery, chopped
1 cup raisins
2 cups vanilla yogurt

Toss the shredded carrots, raisins, and chopped celery together in a large bowl. Stir in the yogurt. Chill before serving.

Heart Smart Snack

In small bowls, have each child combine two tablespoons each of the following ingredients:

toasted oat cereal
raisins
sunflower seeds
low-fat snack crackers

Place this mix on precut 9" x 9" squares of decorative fabric. Gather the sides together and tie with ribbon to make a take-home treat for guests.

Bear-y Good Treats

Two seasonal recipes to prepare with your students as bears come out of their winter hibernations.

Teddy Bear Bread

Use your favorite bread recipe or a quick bread mix. Prepare the dough according to directions. Before baking, divide the dough into eight parts: large ball, medium ball and six small balls. Place the large and medium balls on a greased cookie sheet to form a teddy bear head and body. Flatten the balls slightly. Position four small balls against the body to form paws and two small balls against the top of the head as ears. Press the balls to the sides or edge of the body and head to join them. Flatten the small balls, also. Use raisins to make a face and buttons on the teddy bear. Bake the dough, following the recipe directions. Serve Teddy Bear Bread with butter, jelly and honey.

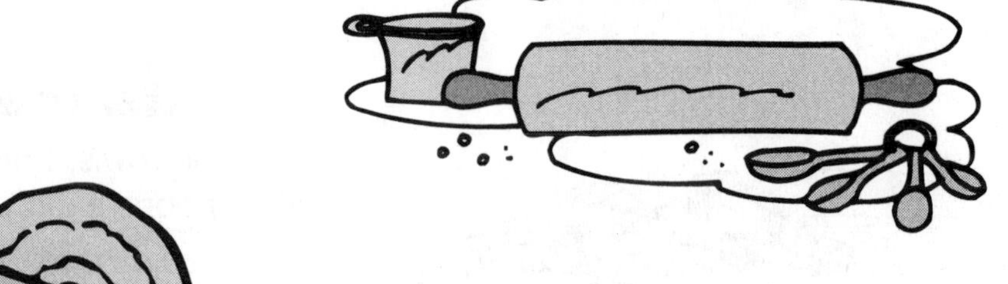

Berry Bear

Ingredients

- English muffins
- peanut butter
- banana, sliced
- grapes
- prunes
- raisins

Toast an English muffin half for each child. Have the children spread their muffin halves with peanut butter. Let each create a bear face by adding banana slice ears, grape eyes, a prune nose and a raisin mouth.

Teddy's Tasty Dessert

Ingredients

- 2 cups graham cracker crumbs
- 1/2 cup melted butter or margarine
- 1 can sweetened condensed milk
- maraschino cherries
- 1/4 cup granulated sugar
- 2 pkg. Dream Whip™
- 6 1/2 oz. can of pink lemonade*
- walnut or pecan slices

Mix the crumbs, sugar and melted butter together. In a 9" x 11" pan, press down 3/4 cup of the mixture. Whip the two packages of Dream Whip™ as directed. Add the condensed milk and lemonade. Whip until blended. Pour over the crumb mixture. Sprinkle with the remaining crumbs. Decorate with cherries and nuts. Cover with plastic wrap and freeze for several hours. (Overnight is best.) Cut to serve. (*You can substitute any frozen juice for the lemonade.)

Honey Bear Sandwiches

Ingredients

- peanut butter
- banana slices
- honey graham crackers
- honey (optional)

Spread peanut butter on a graham cracker. Add a banana slice or two. Top with another cracker or leave it "open face." (For students who are allergic to peanut butter, spread the cracker with honey. For those students who are adventurous, add the honey along with the peanut butter and banana.)

Teddy's Crunch

Ingredients

- miniature colored marshmallows
- peanuts (unsalted)
- honey
- seedless raisins
- coconut

In a large bowl, mix together all the ingredients except the honey. Drizzle the honey over the mixture and toss.

Lucky Pudding

Materials

measuring cup and spoons
pistachio instant pudding
small jars with tops (or cups)
spoons
milk

Preparations

- Decorate a container (big enough to hold pudding) with shamrocks and so on. Label it *Lucky Powder.*
- Put dried pudding in container.
- Copy recipe on chart paper for students to record.

On St. Patrick's Day

Tell children a story about being visited by a leprechaun (make the story as wild as you want). Tell them he left this magic powder with gold nuggets (pistachio nuts) in it. Have students copy the recipe. Then help students follow the recipe. They will notice the MAGIC when the white powder turns green and gets thick! You might want them to write a story to go with their experience.

Recipe for Lucky Irish Pudding

1 baby food or other small jar with lid or paper cups
1 tablespoon Lucky Powder
1/4 cup milk for each child

1. Put the powder and milk in the jar.
2. Put the lid on tight!
3. Shake the jar 50 times!
4. Wait five minutes.
5. Open jar and EAT!

Good and Green!

Paddy's Parfaits

Ingredients

green gelatin
pistachio-flavored instant pudding
clear plastic glasses
1 pint whipping cream
green gummi candy

Have students make up the gelatin according to the package directions. (You may want to make this the day before you plan to use it.) Refrigerate until set. Make up the pudding according to package directions. Whip the cream. Put a couple of spoonfuls of gelatin in each glass. Add a couple of spoonfuls of pudding on top. Place a spoonful of whipped cream on top of the pudding. Top it off with a green gummi candy. Enjoy!

Green Potatoes

Ingredients

potatoes
milk
butter/margarine
grated Parmesan cheese
chopped broccoli or peas

Peel, chop, and boil potatoes. Cool slightly, then allow children to help mash them by hand or with a mixer. Add milk and butter or margarine, as necessary, to reach desired consistency. Steam vegetables, then stir vegetables and grated cheese into potatoes. Serve warm.

Shamus' Shanty

Ingredients

limeade
your favorite ice cream
green maraschino cherries
clear plastic glasses, straws and spoons

Scoop a couple of spoonfuls of ice cream into each glass. Fill glass with limeade. Top with a maraschino cherry. Top of the mornin' to you! (You can substitute ginger ale or lemon-lime soda for the limeade, but my students enjoyed the refreshing taste of the limeade.)

Lucky Green Punch

Pour lime soda into a plastic glass. Add one scoop of mint chip ice cream. Squirt on whipped cream and top with a green maraschino cherry. Sip this punch through a straw. (Serves one.)

Easy Earth Day Cake

Materials

1 box chocolate cake mix
1 can white frosting
blue food coloring
1 small package green Jell-O™
dragees (edible silver balls used for cake decorating)
1 box animal crackers
clean sheet of white paper
2 8" or 9" cake pans
6" plastic bowl

Directions

Bake chocolate cake according to package directions. Let cake cool! If you don't, you will have crumbs littering your Earth! Frost with white icing. (Save about 1 cup of the icing in a separate bowl to use with blue food coloring for the oceans.)

Next, place a plastic bowl (approximately 6") upside down, lightly stenciling a circle in the middle of the cake. Mix blue food coloring into the remaining white icing and frost the round Earth blue.

Cut out the stencil of continents (found on the next page), being careful not to cut into the "oceans." Tape any places together that you might cut. Next, lay your "stencil" on top of the blue Earth frosted on the cake. Sprinkle a light coating of green Jell-O™ over the open stencil. Lift carefully. (Have someone help if possible.) If you do not have any Jell-O™, you could also use white icing mixed with green food coloring and spread over stencil with your finger.

Place animal crackers along edges of cake to represent our endangered species! Use your imagination! Add other decorations to your Earth cake.

Optional: Place a few edible dragees, which are round silver cake-decorating balls, around the universe as stars. Or use silver star decals. Just remember to remove before serving. For a different look, a 13" x 9" pan may be used for the cake.

by Rebecca Kai Dotlich

Earth Day Cake Pattern

Culinary Cuties

.ıd your children to delightful snacks by creating these culinary cuties.

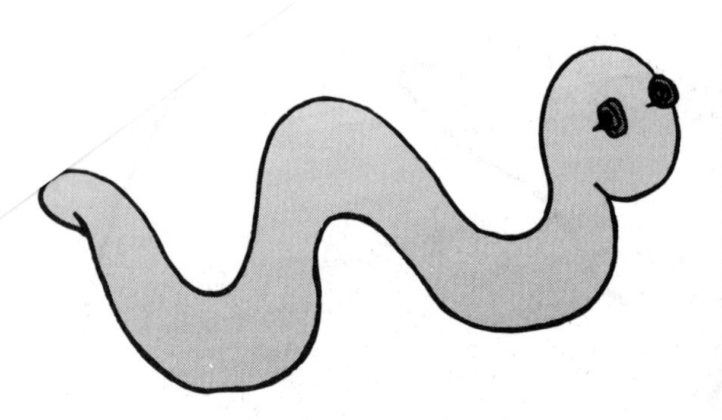

Caterpillar Bread

Ingredients

frozen bread dough, thawed
flour
1/4 c. butter or margarine, melted
raisins
green food coloring

Tint the butter/margarine with green food coloring and set aside. Have children dip a small piece of dough into flour, roll it into a caterpillar shape, then add raisin eyes. Place the caterpillars on a cookie sheet and brush with the green butter/margarine. Bake at 350°F for about 15 minutes.

Caterpickle

Ingredients

cottage cheese
shredded lettuce
sliced pickles
cherry tomatoes
chow mein noodles
green food coloring
toothpicks

Tint the cottage cheese with green food coloring. Stir in shredded lettuce until the mixture resembles grass. Spread a little of the grass mixture on a plate. Use a toothpick to pierce two holes in one cherry tomato; then insert a chow mein noodle antenna in each hole. This will be the head of the caterpillar. Place it on the "grass." Add the caterpillar body by alternating upright pickle slices between cherry tomatoes.

Cheese Caterpillar

Ingredients

1 8-oz. pkg. cream cheese, softened
1 12-oz. pkg. shredded cheddar or American cheese
hives, diced and dried
ow mein noodles
uce leaves

nbine and blend the two cheeses together. Place a lettuce leaf a plate for each child. Have each child form four or five small ese balls, roll the balls in dried chives; then place the balls on the tuce leaf in the shape of a caterpillar. The children can then break chow mein noodles and add them for eyes and antennae.

Sail-Away Snacks

Graham Cracker Raft

Ingredients

graham crackers
applesauce
peanut butter
pretzel sticks

Combine peanut butter and applesauce to make a spreadable, but not runny, mixture. Break graham crackers into squares. Have the children spread the peanut butter mixture over their squares; then add pretzel stick logs across the top.

Celery Sailboats

Ingredients

celery stalks
cottage cheese
leaf lettuce
raisins
red and blue food coloring
toothpicks

Cut celery stalks in half, wash them, and give one to each student. Divide the cottage cheese into three containers. Leave one cottage cheese section white, tint the second one red, and the third one blue. Let the students fill their celery with red, white, and blue cottage cheese. Have each tear a lettuce leaf sail, insert a toothpick mast, then stand the sail in the boat. Add raisin sailors.

Sunshine Snacks and Salads

Sunflower Salad

Ingredients

cottage cheese
cheese slices
leaf lettuce
crushed pineapple, drained
raisins

Place a lettuce leaf on a plate. Combine the cottage cheese with the crushed pineapple. Place a scoop of the cottage cheese mixture on the lettuce leaf. Cut cheese into triangle shapes for flower petals. Place these on the lettuce around the cottage cheese mixture. Press raisin "seeds" into the cottage cheese mixture.

Sun Sandwich

Ingredients

bread
peanut butter
raisins
carrot
celery

Cut a slice of bread into a circle shape. Spread peanut butter over the top. Use two slices of celery to make "happy" eyes. Use one slice of celery to make a smiling mouth. Use a raisin for the nose. Use carrot sticks to surround the bread as rays.

Plate of Sunshine

Ingredients

hard-boiled eggs
mayonnaise
triangle-shaped crackers or toast

Chop the eggs and mix with a little mayonnaise to make egg salad. Place a scoop of egg salad in the center of a plate. Surround this mound of egg salad with triangle-shaped crackers or toast. To eat, scoop up the egg salad with the crackers/toast.

Sunflower Seed Pops

Ingredients

banana
vanilla yogurt
sunflower seeds
craft stick

Slice the banana in half. Insert the craft stick into the flat end. Dip the banana into the yogurt, then roll it in the sunflower seeds.

Special Salads for Spring

Here's a variety of simple and fun spring salads to welcome spring!

Pastel Fruit Salad

Ingredients

1 large can pineapple chunks, drained
1 can mandarin oranges, drained
1 small jar Maraschino cherries, drained
1 cup flaked coconut
1 cup pastel-colored marshmallows
1 to 2 cups sour cream (enough to coat)

Mix all the ingredients together and refrigerate. Serve in clear plastic cups for all the pretty colors to show through.

Note: The recipe may need to be doubled or tripled according to class size.

Bunny Salad

Rabbits are famous for eating carrots. Make and serve a favorite carrot-raisin salad with your students.

Ingredients

4 cups grated carrots
1 cup raisins
1/2 cup mayonnaise or Miracle Whip™

Grate the carrots. Put all the ingredients into a bowl. Mix well and refrigerate till serving time. Put a scoop onto a lettuce leaf and serve with crackers.

Marshmallow Milk

Serve a cup of warm milk with a floating chocolate-covered marshmallow egg. Use a small straw to stir and sip.

by Tania Kourempis-Cowling

Fruit Bunny Salad

Ingredients

lettuce, shredded
cottage cheese
applesauce
cinnamon
peach slices
blueberries
strawberry pieces
banana sticks

Combine equal amounts of applesauce and cottage cheese. Mix well. Stir in a sprinkle of cinnamon. Refrigerate this mixture for several hours or overnight. To make the bunny, spread shredded lettuce over a plate and top with a scoop of the applesauce mixture for the head. Place two peach slice rabbit ears above the head. Add blue-berry eyes, a strawberry piece nose and banana stick whiskers.

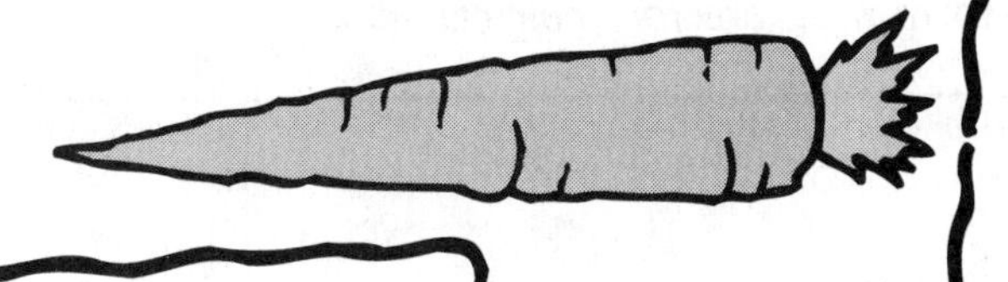

Salad Bundles

Ingredients

carrots
celery
cucumbers
lettuce leaves
plastic wrap

Cut the carrots, celery and cucumbers into sticks. Have the children count out two of each and place the collection on a lettuce leaf. Let them roll up the lettuce leaf to create their own portable salads. Help them wrap the bundles in plastic wrap. Carry these outside on a nice day for a picnic snack.

by Marie E. Cecchini

Easy Easter Recipes

Invite parents to a pre-Easter breakfast and serve these fun-to-prepare easy recipes.

Bunny Breakfast

Ingredients

English muffins
cream cheese
grape jam
strawberry jam
mandarin oranges
craft sticks

Toast an English muffin for each child. Cool to the touch; then spread both halves of muffin with cream cheese to make a white rabbit. Cut one of each child's muffin halves into two pieces. Place the muffin round on a plate for the rabbit face. Place the two muffin pieces above the face for ears. Spoon on strawberry jam eyes and a grape jam nose. Demonstrate for the children how to place a craft stick into the grape jam; then pull it through the cream cheese to form whiskers for their rabbits.

Colorful Scrambled Eggs

Ingredients

1 dozen or more eggs
(according to class size)
food coloring
margarine to coat frying pans

Crack the eggs into a mixing bowl. Whip the eggs thoroughly. Divide the mixture into several bowls. Add a drop or two of food coloring; use green, blue and red. You will need several frying pans to cook the colored eggs separately. Serve a small scoop of scrambled eggs in each color along with buttered toast strips.

Bunny Bird Gorp

A handful of this irresistible mix means crunchy-coated popcorn and a menagerie of gummy bunnies and jelly bird eggs.

Ingredients
6 cups popped popcorn
1 cup dry roasted peanuts
1/2 cup brown sugar
1/4 cup margarine
2 tablespoons honey
1/2 teaspoon ground cinnamon
Gummy bunnies and jelly bird eggs

Place the popcorn and peanuts in a greased 15" x 10" x 1" baking pan. In saucepan, combine brown sugar, margarine, honey and cinnamon. Cook and stir over low heat until boiling. Continue boiling for about 4 minutes. Pour over the popcorn mixture and stir to coat.

Now, bake the mixture in a 300° oven for about 20 minutes (stirring frequently). Transfer the cooled mixture into a large bowl, adding the bunnies and jelly beans. Serve or make treat bags!

Easter Cupcake Cones

Ingredients
1 box yellow cake mix
30-36 flat bottom ice-cream cones
1 can vanilla frosting
food coloring
cake sprinkles and small jelly beans

Prepare the cake mix according to package directions. Fill each ice-cream cone with cake batter to within 3/4" of the top. Place the cones in a baking pan and carefully bake them in a 350° oven for 20-25 minutes or until a toothpick inserted comes out clean. Cool completely.

Decide which color you would like to frost your cupcake cones. Use a drop or two of food coloring to change the vanilla frosting into pink, yellow or lilac.

red with frosting = pink
yellow with frosting = pastel yellow
red and blue with frosting = lilac

Decorate with sprinkles or jelly beans!

Edible Easter Baskets

Graham Cracker Basket

An easy-to-make basket can be made by adapting the graham cracker "gingerbread house."

Materials

graham crackers broken into squares (5 for each child)
frosting "glue" (1 lb. powdered sugar, 3 egg whites, $1/2$ tsp. cream of tartar)
cake frosting (white, pink, green or yellow)
small decorations (sprinkles, M&M's®, candy "flowers," jelly beans)
shoestring licorice cut in 6" lengths (1 piece for each child)

Directions

Lay one cracker square flat. Line the edges with frosting "glue." One square at a time, frost edges and fit them onto the base, forming a square box. Let dry until the next day! (Hint: If it is too difficult to get the sides to stand up, make it upside down, forming it over a greased or sprayed lunch milk carton. The carton can be removed easily once the "glue" has dried.)

One side at a time, frost the graham squares, decorating them with the sprinkles, etc. Put a ball of frosting "glue" at the top of two opposite sides and insert the shoestring licorice "handle." Let dry.

Fill baskets with *lightweight* candies such as marshmallow chicks, chocolate-covered pretzels, individually wrapped LifeSavers®.

Biscuit Dough Basket

Materials

biscuit dough (prepared or a box mix)
non-stick spray
shoestring licorice or ribbons (cut in 8" lengths)
regular size cupcake tins

Directions

Invert cupcake tins and spray with non-stick spray. Form dough over inverted cupcake tins. Bake at given heat. Before dough is cooled, poke two holes across from each other toward the top. When cooled, insert either licorice or ribbon for handles. Let cool completely before filling. Older children might cut the dough into strips and weave or crisscross them over the inverted cupcake forms.

Fill with small candies, miniature marshmallows, raisins or even trail mix.

Note: Prepared pie crust can also be used, if "baskets" are filled with pudding or pie filling.

PURIM IS SPECIAL

Every year on Purim, Jewish children will hear the story of Queen Esther. With the help of her cousin, Mordecai, Esther saved the Jews from the plan of Haman, a wicked man who tried to have all the Jews killed.

The story is read by the rabbi from a special scroll called a Megillah. Every time Haman's name is read, the children whirl noisemakers, stamp their feet and make a lot of noise so Haman's name can't be heard. It is the only time that noise can be made in the synagogue or temple.

Purim is a happy holiday. Children dress up in costumes and have parades and parties. They eat Hamantaschen, a special three-cornered cookie filled with jelly. It reminds the children of Haman's three-cornered hat.

Purim is also a time to share. Gifts of Hamantaschen, cookies, fruit and candy are given to family and friends. Special baskets of food and toys are given to people who are poor, sick or lonely. Money is collected or raised at the Purim carnival and given to charities.

Jews all over the world look forward to this happy holiday!

Hamantaschen Recipe

Try this special Purim treat! Makes about 4 dozen Hamantaschen.

1 cup sugar
1/3 cup oil
1/3 cup shortening
3 eggs
1/2 cup orange juice

4 cups flour
3 tsp. baking powder
1 tsp. salt
1 egg, beaten
jelly or canned prune mix for filling

PROCESS:

1. Cream the sugar, oil and shortening.
2. Add the 3 eggs and juice. Mix well.
3. Blend with the dry ingredients. Roll into a ball.
4. Divide into 4 parts. Roll out each piece very thin (about 1/8") on a floured board.
5. With the rim of a cup or glass, cut into the dough to make circles.
6. Place 1/2 to 2/3 teaspoon of filling in the middle of each circle.
7. Shape into a triangle—lift up right and left sides of circle, leaving the bottom side down. Bring both sides to meet at the center, above the filling. Lift the bottom side up to meet the other two sides.
8. Preheat oven to 350°F. Brush the dough with beaten egg before baking.
9. Place on a greased cookie sheet. Bake approximately 20 minutes.

by Judy Wolfman

Celebrate Passover

During passover, Jews all over the world will sit down to a special meal called a seder to celebrate their freedom.

Many years ago, Jews lived in Egypt, where the King was very cruel. The Jews became his slaves and worked hard making bricks for the King's buildings.

A young man, Moses, felt sorry for the Jews, and went to the King many times to ask him to let the Jewish slaves go free. But the King refused, and made them work harder.

God helped Moses by bringing on 10 plagues to the King. The tenth one brought the angel of death, who killed
the firstborn in every Egyptian home but passed over the homes of the Jews. (This is where the name *Passover* comes from.)

The King finally let the Jews go. Moses told them to pack quickly, led them out of Egypt, the land of slavery, to a land of freedom.

The *seder,* which means a particular order of service that goes with the meal, has special foods that help today's Jews remember the story of Passover.

The *matzoh* is like a cracker and is very flat. It reminds the Jews that they left Egypt in such a hurry that their bread didn't have time to rise and bake properly.

Moror, or bitter herbs like horseradish, reminds the Jews of how bitter it was to be slaves.

A mixture of apples, nuts, cinnamon and wine, called *charoses* is a reminder of the mortar and bricks the Jews made for the King.

Parsley, a reminder of spring, is dipped in salt water to make the Jews think of the tears that were shed when they were hardworking slaves.

Two other foods, a roasted egg and a roasted lamb bone, recall the special sacrifices that were made.

While families enjoy this religious dinner together, they read from a special book called the Haggadah. Everyone participates as they share the story of Passover.

A mixture of apples, nuts, cinnamon and wine, called *charoses* is a reminder of the mortar and bricks the Jews made for the King.

by Judy Wolfman

Passover Traditions

These traditional Passover recipes are simple to prepare. Introduce your students to ***matzo brei*** (fried matzo) which is a favorite breakfast treat and to ***charoses***, a staple of the seder table.

Matzo Brei

Ingredients

matzo (1/2 piece per student)
eggs (1 egg for each full piece of matzo)
butter
sugar boiling water

Boil 3-4 cups of water. Break matzo into bite-size pieces and place in glass bowl. In a separate bowl, break eggs and beat. Once water has boiled, pour over broken matzo and allow to sit for one minute or until matzo has softened slightly. Melt butter in frying pan. Drain water from matzo. Add beaten eggs to coat matzo. When butter has melted, add matzo-egg mixture and cook to brown turning frequently to get crispy. Serve and sprinkle sugar on top of fried matzo.

Charoses

Ingredients

1 cup apples, peeled and chopped
1/4 cup chopped nuts
1 teaspoon honey
1 teaspoon cinnamon
grated rind of 1/2 lemon (optional)
2 tablespoons of red wine (or grape juice)

Mix all of the ingredients together in a bowl. Serve with matzoh or crackers. Makes a tasty snack!

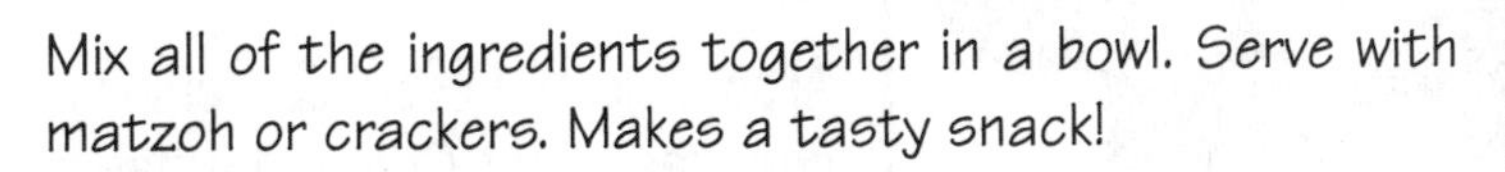

You may need someone to help you chop the apples and nuts.

Celebrate Cinco de Mayo!

Tortillas

Tortillas are a staple food of Mexico. Purchase these in the dairy case of your supermarket. Cook on a hot griddle or electric skillet in a small amount of oil. Turn frequently. Spread with cheese and roll up.

Cinco de Mayo Salad

1 head lettuce, shredded
1 pound cheddar cheese, grated
3 tomatoes, cubed
1 onion, chopped
1 large package corn chips
1 pound ground chuck, browned
1 1/4 package taco seasoning mix
2 cups red kidney beans, drained

Using a plastic knife, allow the children to shred, grate, cube and chop the ingredients. (Always watch children closely when using knives.) Toss vegetables and corn chips. Have ground chuck already prepared or do this yourself. Stir in taco seasoning and beans. Parents, children and other guests can make individual servings. Serves 25 to 30.

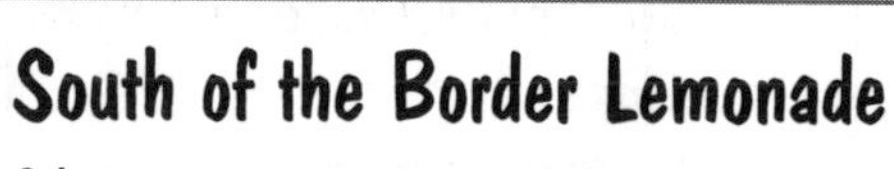

South of the Border Lemonade

6 lemons
1 1/2 cups sugar
2 1/2 quarts water

Allow children to squeeze lemons, making sure each child has a turn. Combine water, sugar and juice in a gallon container. Stir until well blended. Serve over ice. Makes 3 quarts.

Note: You may want to ask room parents to contribute enchiladas, refried beans and tacos for guests and children to sample during your Cinco de Mayo celebration.

Banana Tacos

Ingredients

instant banana pudding
banana slices
milk
taco shells

Prepare the pudding with milk as directed on the package. Chill. Spoon pudding into taco shells, then push banana slices into the pudding.

Mexican Hot Chocolate

Ingredients

1 teaspoon cocoa
3 teaspoons sugar
1/3 cup powdered milk
1/2 teaspoon cinnamon

Fill the cup with hot water and stir. You can add a squirt of whipped cream if you wish!

Fruit Tacos

Ingredients

2 1 lb. 4 oz. cans pineapple chunks
2 16 oz. cans mandarin oranges
2 8 oz. containers strawberry yogurt
1 7 oz. package flaked coconut
taco shells

Drain the fruit well. Pour it into a large mixing bowl. Add the yogurt and coconut. Stir well to combine and coat the fruit with yogurt. Spoon the mixture into taco shells.

Rainy Day Snack

Ingredients

tortillas
refried beans
shredded lettuce
grated cheese
bread sticks
prepared salsa

Tear the tortillas in half to form umbrella shapes. Have children top their umbrellas with a small amount of refried beans, shredded lettuce, and grated cheese; then place half of a bread stick at the bottom as a handle. To eat, let children roll up their tortillas and dip their bread sticks in salsa.

Make These for Mother's Day!

Two recipes to treat mothers to! Invite mothers to join the class for a special Mother's Day breakfast and serve Sunshine Muffins. Children can practice making this ahead of time using colored construction paper shapes to create the sunshine muffin. Or bake almond cookies a day ahead and serve with tea after lunch.

Sunshine Muffins

Ingredients

English muffin halves
cream cheese
cheese slices
pineapple slices
raisins
yellow food coloring

Toast the muffin halves and tint the cream cheese with yellow food coloring. Place each muffin half on a plate. Top the muffin halves with yellow cream cheese. Break or cut the cheese slices into triangle sun rays, and place the triangles around each muffin. Set raisin eyes, a raisin nose and a half slice pineapple smile into the cream cheese.

Almond Cookies

Ingredients

1 cup margarine
1 cup sugar
2 eggs
1 teaspoon almond extract
2 1/2 cups flour (sifted)
1/4 teaspoon baking sodaO
roasted almonds

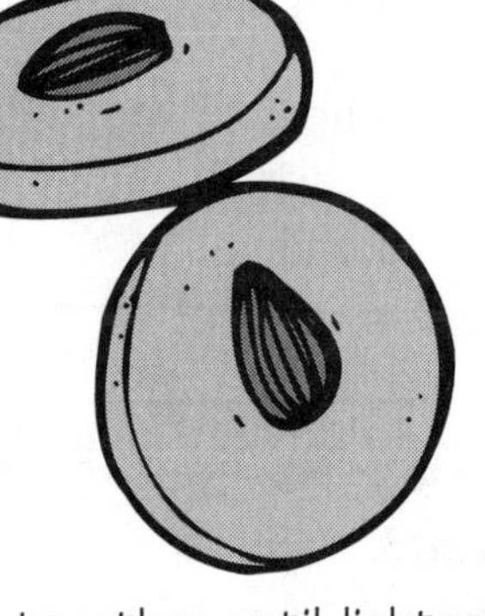

Beat margarine and sugar together until light and fluffy. Add one egg and the almond extract. Mix. Slowly add flour and baking soda. Chill this dough before shaping. Shape walnut-sized balls of dough with your hands. Press the ball flat on an ungreased cookie sheet. Brush the cookies with the other egg (beaten), pressing an almond into the center of each cookie.

Bake the cookies for about 20 minutes in a 350°F oven, checking the last few minutes for doneness. All ovens vary; you may need more or less time. Cool and enjoy!

Singing to Mom

Teach children this simple little song so they can go home and sing it to their mothers at the breakfast or tea.

To the tune of "Twinkle, Twinkle, Little Star"

Do I love you? Yes I do,
And I'm thankful just for you.
You are what a mom should be,
Working hard and helping me,
Showing love in all you do.
Thank you, Mom. I love you, too.

Mother's Day Place Mat

1. Children decorate two large white paper doilies with colorful artwork.
2. Glue the doilies on a 12" x 18" sheet of red or pink construction paper.
3. Cover with clear self-adhesive plastic, if you wish.
4. Decorate a film container with stickers and glitter.
5. Use hot glue to attach the container to the top left corner of the place mat. (You'll need adult help with the glue gun.)
6. Make small paper flowers, or collect small twigs to put in each vase. Use the place mats for Mother's Day breakfast or tea.

Hot and Cold Spring Drinks

Sometimes a spring day can be warm and lovely. Sometimes it can feel like winter! Here are two drinks to prepare and enjoy depending on the weather.

Honey Hot Chocolate

Ingredients (for each cup)
1/4 cup water
pinch of salt
1 T. unsweetened cocoa

Add:
1 tablespoon honey
3/4 cup milk
Heat, but do not boil.

Milk 'n' Honey Punch

Ingredients (serves 6)
6 eggs
3/4 cup honey
1/2 tsp. ground nutmeg
1 quart milk

Beat eggs until they are foamy. Gradually pour honey into egg mixture. Stir nutmeg into milk. Heat on low heat, but do not allow to boil. Allow to cool and serve.

Favorite Spring Recipes

As you find new recipes, cut and attach them to this page for future use.

Summer Surprises

This variety of critters, clowns, and other cute surprises will delight your students from spring right through summer. Plan in advance to prepare and serve for an indoor lunch or enjoy outdoors, picnic style!

Lucky Clover Snack

Ingredients

- cucumber slices
- celery sticks
- cream cheese
- green food color

Tint the cream cheese with food color. Place a dollop of cream cheese in the center of a plate. Wedge four cucumber slices into the cream cheese to resemble a four-leaf clover. Insert a celery stick at the bottom for a stem.

Daisy Delight

Ingredients

- hard-boiled egg slices
- mayonnaise
- celery sticks
- cheese slices
- yellow food color
- paprika

Tint the mayonnaise with food color. Place a small amount of mayonnaise on a plate. Surround the mayonnaise with egg slices to make the blossom. Set a celery stick at the bottom of the blossom for a stem. Cut a cheese slice diagonally, forming two triangles. Place a triangle at either side of the stem as a leaf. Sprinkle paprika over the mayonnaise.

The Cracker Family

Ingredients

- crackers, assorted shapes
- carrot sticks
- dry cereal shapes
- raisins
- peanut butter
- cheese slice
- sunflower seeds

Spread peanut butter on a round cracker and place it on a plate for a head. Choose a second cracker shape for the body and spread peanut butter on it. Use additional peanut butter as glue and add carrot stick arms and legs to the cracker body. Tear several small pieces from the cheese slice and place them at the top of the head for hair. Use dry cereal pieces, raisins, currants, sunflower seeds and so on to make a family and to decorate the bodies. Make a whole "Cracker Family."

Bee Bites

Ingredients

cottage cheese
carrot shavings
cheese slices
toasted bread
yellow food color
whole cloves

Tint the cottage cheese with food color. Place two mounds of cottage cheese on a plate, elongating the second mound. Use a blunt knife to cut six cheese-strip legs. Lay three cheese strips on either side of the cottage cheese. Place carrot-shaving stripes along the bee's body. Rip or cut four wing shapes from toast and insert these into the cottage cheese, two on each side. Insert the "ball" end of a whole clove into the bottom for a "stinger." Insert the narrow ends of two cloves into the head for antennae. Cloves are for ornamental purposes only.

Roly-Poly Caterpillar

Ingredients

bread slices
cream cheese
green grapes
green food color

Tint the cream cheese with food color. Cut a bread slice into a leaf shape, then cover it with green cream cheese. Set grapes "bumper to bumper" along the bread leaf to resemble a caterpillar.

Dandy Dragonfly

Ingredients

cucumber slices
bananas
carrot sticks
bread slices
cream cheese
carrot curls

Set two cucumber slices, vertically, on a plate. Peel and halve the banana, then cut each banana half lengthwise. Place one banana section below the cucumber slices, narrow end at plate bottom. Place three carrot sticks on either side of this dragonfly body, and two carrot curls at the head for antennae. Cut or rip bread into four wing shapes. Spread cream cheese over each wing, and lay two wing shapes on either side of the dragonfly.

Tasty Turtle

Ingredients

cottage cheese
green food coloring
green grapes
raisins
cheese slices

Tint the cottage cheese green with the food coloring. Place a mound of green cottage cheese onto the center of a plate for the turtle shell. Push a green grape slightly into the cottage cheese for a head. Add two raisins to each side of the cottage cheese mound as legs. Cut a small triangle from a cheese slice and add it to the back of the turtle for a tail.

Beehive Snack

Ingredients

empty egg cartons (Styrofoam™ type)
$1\frac{1}{2}$ to 2 cups rice cereal
1 cup peanut butter
$\frac{1}{3}$ cup honey
$\frac{1}{2}$ to $\frac{3}{4}$ cup raisins (bees)

Mix these ingredients together (it will be sticky). Mold and press the mixture into the sections of the egg cartons (greasing your hands with butter will help). Chill in the freezer till firm. Pop out these little beehives and enjoy!

Ladybug Sundae

A tasty way to learn about insects is by creating your own snack. You will need strawberry ice cream or frozen yogurt, pitted prunes, raisins, and black string licorice. Provide each child with one scoop of ice cream or yogurt for the ladybug body; then have them add a prune head and raisin spots. Tear six pieces of black string licorice to place around the ice cream/yogurt for legs and two more near the top of the head for antennae. Happy snacking!

Jiggling Octopus

Ingredients

orange-flavored gelatin
raisins
carrot strips
fish-shaped crackers

Prepare orange gelatin according to package directions. Pour the gelatin into a long pan (9" x 13" or a similar size). When the gelatin is set, use a round cookie cutter or a water glass to cut circular gelatin shapes. Lay the gelatin circles in the middle of a plate (blue plates are especially well suited). Push 8 thin carrot strips into the gelatin as octopus tentacles. Add raisin eyes to the gelatin. Sprinkle fish-shaped crackers around the plate. Each child can make their own Jiggling Octopus or cut a large gelatin circle and make one octopus for the group to share.

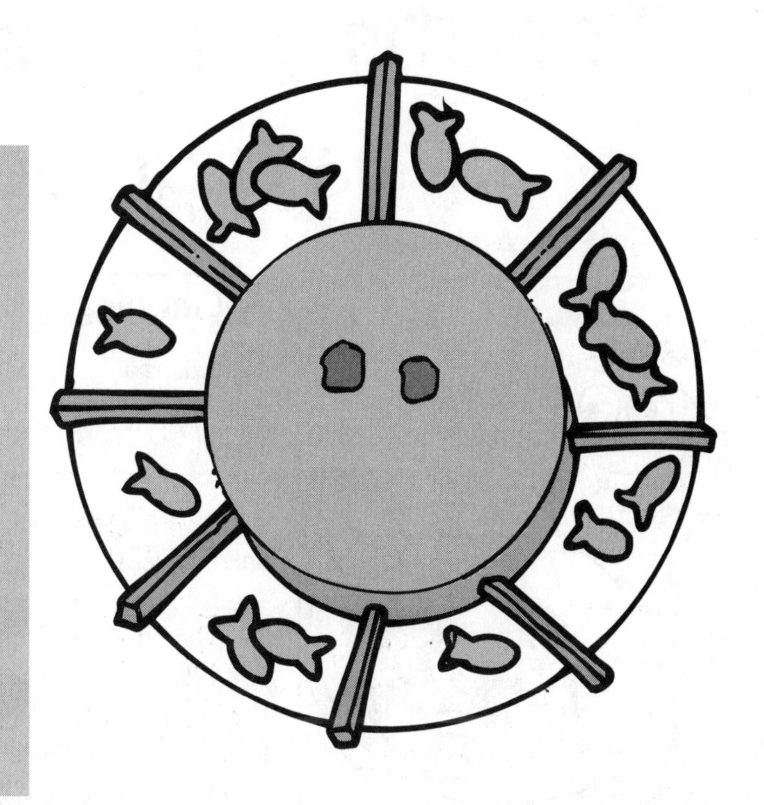

Octopus Snack

Ingredients

cottage cheese
grapes
carrot sticks
apple slices
raisins

Invite your class to craft octopus snacks. First center a scoop of cottage cheese on a plate for each child. Have the children place eight carrot stick "tentacles" around the cottage cheese mound. Let them add raisin eyes, a grape nose, and an apple slice mouth.

Sometimes playing with food is a good idea!

Clowning Around

Ingredients

pita bread
carrot shavings
cherry tomatoes
(whole and sliced)
carrot slices
wheat bread
strawberries, chunked
sandwich spreads
(egg or tuna salad and so on)

Cut the pita bread open to form two circles. Cover one circle with sandwich spread and set it on a plate. Sprinkle carrot shaving hair at the top of the circle. Set two carrot slices into the sandwich spread for eyes. Add a cherry tomato nose and two cherry tomato slices for cheeks. Form a mouth with strawberry chunks. Cut a triangle shape from the wheat bread. Cover the triangle with a different sandwich spread. Set the triangle at the top of the head for a hat. Top the hat with a whole cherry tomato pom-pom.

Funny Faces

Ingredients

bread slices
peanut butter
cream cheese
shredded carrots
raisins
cherries, halved
strawberry slices
blueberries

Cut or tear one bread slice into a circle. Spread cream cheese over the circle and place it on a plate. Create a clown face by adding raisin eyes, a cherry half nose, strawberry slice cheeks, a blueberry mouth, and shredded carrot hair. Cut or tear a second bread slice into a triangle. Spread peanut butter over the triangle. Place this at the top of the clown face for a hat. Add a cherry half pom-pom to the top of the hat.

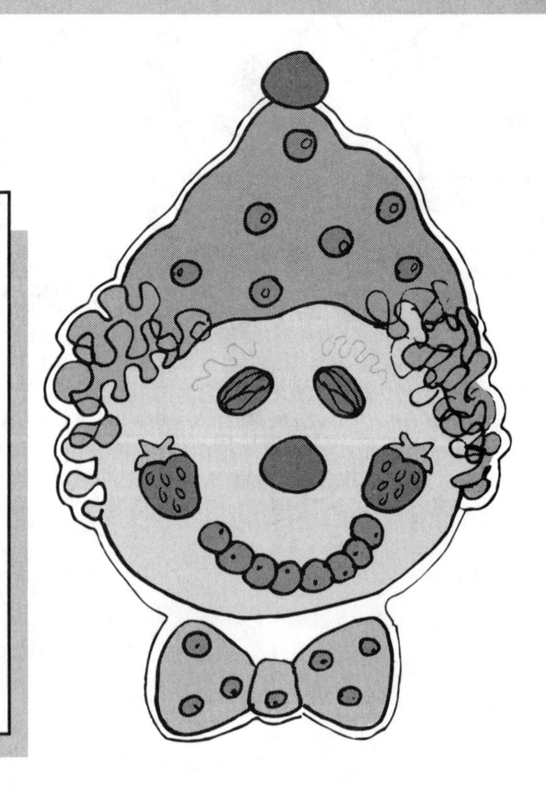

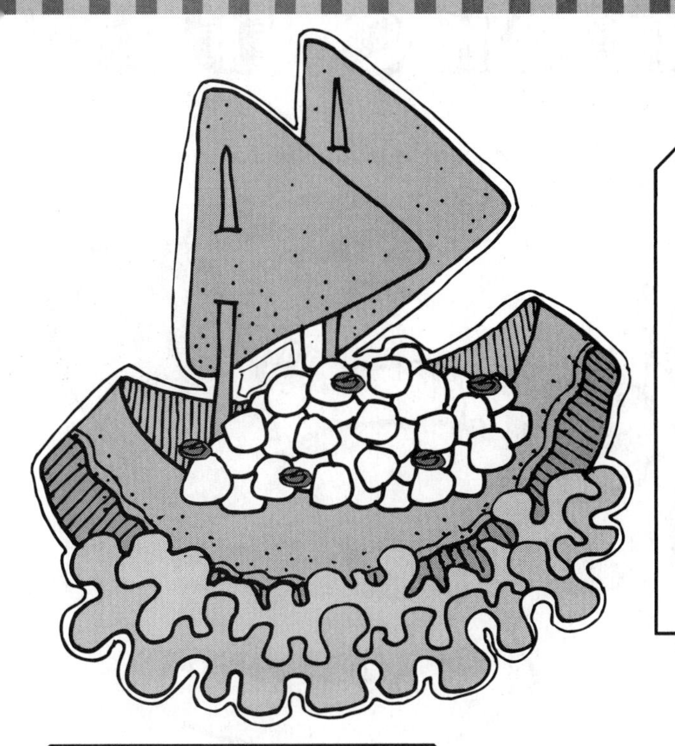

Melon Boats

Ingredients

melon slices
cottage cheese
raisins
cheese slices
leaf lettuce
toothpicks

Place a lettuce leaf on a plate. Set a melon slice onto the lettuce. Spoon cottage cheese into the center of the melon. Add raisins to the cottage cheese to represent people. Break cheese slices into two triangles. Slide one toothpick into each cheese triangle sail. Place one sail at either end of the melon boat.

Delightful Daisy

Ingredients

sliced pineapple
celery stalk
apple slices
strawberries
lettuce leaf

Place one pineapple slice near the top of a plate. Set a whole strawberry in the center hole. Surround the pineapple with apple slice "petals." Slice the celery stalk lengthwise and place one piece below the pineapple for a flower stem. Tear pieces from a lettuce leaf and set them beside the celery stem for leaves.

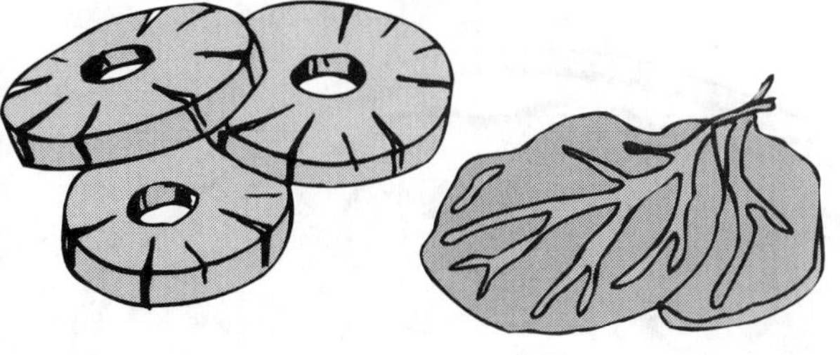

Fruit Tree Salad

Ingredients

cottage cheese
fruit cocktail, drained
toasted bread
green food color

Rip a piece of toast into a tree trunk shape and set it on a plate. Tint the cottage cheese with food color and spread above the toast to resemble a treetop. Set individual pieces of fruit cocktail into the cottage cheese.

Fun for Father's Day

Prepare this delightful sandwich-by-the-sea with your students in class. Encourage students to re-create it at home as a treat for their dads on Father's Day.

By the Seaside Sandwich

Ingredients

1 slice bread (white, wheat, rye, or raisin)
1 tablespoon peanut butter
1 tablespoon grape jelly
3 or 4 bite-size fish-shaped crackers
rolled fruit leather
graham snack teddy bear-shaped cookies
sweetened fruit-flavored round cereal

Spread peanut butter onto one half of the top of the bread slice to create the "beach." Spread grape jelly on the opposite half to create the "ocean." Arrange fish crackers in the ocean. Cut small rectangles from fruit leather to simulate "beach towel" and place on the beach. Top each towel with graham teddy bear cookie. Add fruity cereal rings next to towels.

Dad's Delight Snack Mix

Possible Ingredients

popped corn
nuts
dry cereal
croutons
pretzels
sunflower seeds
chocolate chips
raisins
shredded coconut
mini marshmallows
sandwich-size plastic bags
ribbon

Directions

1. Set out the ingredients in individual bowls. Place a serving spoon or small scoop in each bowl.
2. Provide each child with a small plastic bag. Instruct children to create their own special snack mix for Father's Day.
3. Seal each bag with a twist tie and a ribbon bow. Note: You may want to ask parents to donate the items for this project.

June Juice Jamboree

Invite children to bring in boxes of fruit juice. Check to be sure there is a box for each child. On a warm sunny day, have recess outdoors with children enjoying their juice snack. Serve whole fruits such as apples, grapes, and oranges that are the same as the fruit juices. Save fruit juice boxes. Rinse and use for the following craft activity.

Let's Make It

1. Have an adult assist children as each pokes a hole through the top center of the juice box using a nail.
2. Children will poke their straws through the holes and push them down until they reach the bottom of the boxes.
3. Measure the length of straw protruding from the top of each box.
4. On the plastic sheet, each child draws a rectangular sail with the long side about 1" (2.5 cm) shorter than the straw.
5. Measure to find the center of the rectangle. Mark the center spot at the top and bottom of the "sail."
6. Use the hole punch to make holes on the center spots for the straw to pass through.
7. Decorate the sail and the juice box with fabric paints and stickers and allow them to dry thoroughly.
8. Thread the straw through the holes on the sail so the sail will stand upright.
9. Plan a boat regatta in a water table or wading pool. Your regatta can include a parade of boats, boat races, and an on-the-water obstacle course using floating toys and ice cubes. Boats can be powered with long straws blown by the owners onto the sails. Take this opportunity to talk about force!

Materials

empty juice box
plastic sheet (clear packaging discards, plastic report covers, etc.)
sturdy straw
hole punch
scissors
large nail
fabric paints and stickers

Fun and Fruity

A delightful array of summer snowflakes, soup, salads, and other surprises to make learning seem like a party!

Summer Snowflakes

Ingredients
large marshmallows
fruit chunks (fresh or canned)
toothpicks

Have each child insert toothpicks into the sides of a marshmallow. Then let them choose various chunks of fruit to stick onto the opposite end of each toothpick.

Cold Fruit Soup

Combine three cups of orange juice and one cup of pineapple juice. To the juice, add two cups each of grape halves, orange sections cut in thirds, strawberry halves, and pineapple chunks. Chill. Top each bowl of fruit soup with a cherry. Try cubed melon, peaches, and strawberry halves in an orange juice and cranberry juice mixture.

Stop and Go Salad

Invite children to bring in toy cars from home. Prepare red and green, or red, green, and yellow salad treats. Some combinations to try: strawberries, kiwi, and bananas; watermelon, honeydew, and pineapple; cherries, green grapes, and peaches.

Picnic

Celebrate the warm weather by experimenting with melons, a favorite summer picnic food. You will need a watermelon, cantaloupe, honeydew melon, paper plates, a knife (for adult use) and spoons. Display the uncut melons and have the children compare the differences in color, size and shape. Invite them to feel and smell each melon. Cut each melon in half and again compare the differences. Scoop the seeds from each onto separate paper plates. Invite the children to scoop out a portion of each melon onto a paper plate for tasting. Have the children choose the melon they like best and graph the class results. Which melon was the favorite of the class?

Wonderful Watermelon

A summer favorite, these delightful ideas will make wonderful watermelon even more popular!

Make a Watermelon Butterfly

Easy to make and pretty to look at, this special dessert is perfect for summer cooking activities.

Ingredients

1 slice watermelon (1/2 round per student)
1 lettuce leaf
1 peeled carrot
3 strawberries cut in half
4 raisins

Cut each half slice of watermelon in half. Cut off rind; then cut off a small piece from the top triangle point of each slice to form two wings. Place a leaf of lettuce on a plate. Place two watermelon quarters on lettuce forming butterfly wings. Place a carrot between the wings to form the body. Place three strawberry halves, flat side down, on each wing. Place two raisins on the end of two toothpicks and insert at top of carrot for antennae.

Watermelon Sherbet

watermelon-flavored (or any pink sherbet)
chocolate chips

Place block of sherbet in a large bowl and allow sherbet to soften for easy mixing. Add one cup of chocolate chips and stir well to distribute chips. Repack tightly in original rectangle carton or place in rectangle glass pan and freeze until firm. Cut into slices; then into watermelon-shaped triangle wedges.

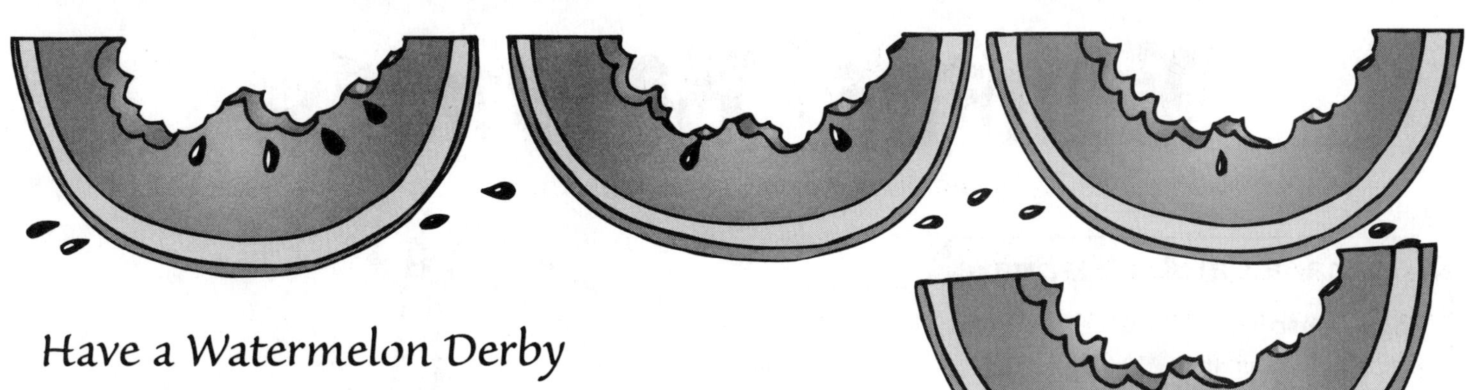

Have a Watermelon Derby

This fun but very messy eating contest is a fun outdoor activity. Be sure children bring an apron or smock to cover themselves during this "no-hands allowed" event! Girls should have their hair tied back so it doesn't get in the way.

You'll need:
- one thick slice of watermelon per child
- napkins and paper towels
- table covered with plastic
- paper plates

For this event, place five to six plates–each with a thick slice of watermelon that will stand upright–on table. Five to six children at a time "race" to see who can finish the slice of watermelon first with hands kept behind their backs. This is a "no hands allowed" event. It's a face-in-the-watermelon race. If the watermelon tips over, children may use their hands to fix it. They just have to bend lower to finish their slice!

Run this event like a race–ready-set-go! Announce the winner of each round. Award prizes to winners if you wish.

Watermelon Dough

Invite the class to help you make watermelon playdough. After it cools, place small amounts into plastic sandwich bags and tie with green ribbon for the children to take home.

- 2 c. flour
- 1 c. salt
- 2 c. water
- 2 T. cooking oil
- 4 T. cream of tartar
- 1 pkg. sugar-free watermelon-flavored gelatin

Place all of the ingredients into a saucepan. Stir constantly over medium heat until the mixture forms a ball. Remove from heat and cool.

Banana Bonanzas

Banana Carob Milk Shake

Ingredients

For each serving:
3/4 cup chilled skim milk
1 tablespoon carob powder
1/3 frozen banana
1/4 teaspoon vanilla extract

Add all ingredients in a blender or shaker. Blend together until smooth and foamy.
Note: If a shaker is used, substitute mashed ripe banana so that it will mix with the other ingredients. Shake until foamy.
A milk shake can be made for snacktime instead of serving plain milk. Other fruits could be substituted for the banana with the children creating their own recipes.

Chocolate Bananas

Ingredients

1 lb. melting chocolate
bananas (1/2 per child)

Cut each banana in half to create two frozen treat shapes. Insert wooden sticks into cut flat ends of bananas. Melt chocolate in a double boiler or heavy saucepan over very low heat. Do not allow chocolate to scald or burn. Let cool about 5 minutes. Dip each banana in melted chocolate turning to coat completely. Place chocolate-coated bananas on a baking sheet lined with waxed paper and place in freezer for about one hour. Remove from freezer and wait about 10 minutes before serving.

Banana-Coconut Sundae

Ingredients

ice cream
bananas
whipped cream
maraschino cherries
flaked coconut

Sprinkle coconut over a plate. Top with a scoop of ice cream. Use a craft stick to form a hole in the center of the ice cream. Insert half a banana, flat side down, into the hole. Spoon a small amount of whipped cream on the top of the banana and top with a cherry.

Ambrosia Salad with Bananas

Ingredients

Salad: raw fruits such as apple, banana, peach, blueberry, strawberry, cantaloupe, watermelon, nectarine, orange, and pear

Ambrosia Dressing:
- 1 cup vanilla-flavored yogurt
- 1/2 cup crushed pineapple
- 1/2 cup shredded coconut
- lettuce leaves or sprouts

Wash fruit. Cut, peel, seed, or hull fruit. Arrange fruit in an interesting design on lettuce leaves or sprouts in a salad plate. Mix yogurt, pineapple and coconut in a bowl. Spoon dressing over fruit. Garnish with berries or sprouts.

Make fruity serving bowls for the fruit salad by scooping out cantaloupe, orange or grapefruit halves, or watermelon sections. Omit lettuce. Add dressing and garnish as in recipe.

Patriotic Palate Pleasers

★ Colonial Muffins ★

Use your favorite muffin mix. Fold in fresh blueberries and chopped strawberries. Bake according to directions. Serve muffins with toothpick decorations.

Buy or make small flags. Adhere two flag stickers back to back with a toothpick in between. You can also use the same procedure with star stickers.

★ Perky Punch ★

Prior to serving, make a tray of ice cubes using several drops of red or blue food coloring in the water. Freeze. Serve apple juice or lemon-lime soda with the colorful ice cubes.

★ Patriotic Popcorn ★

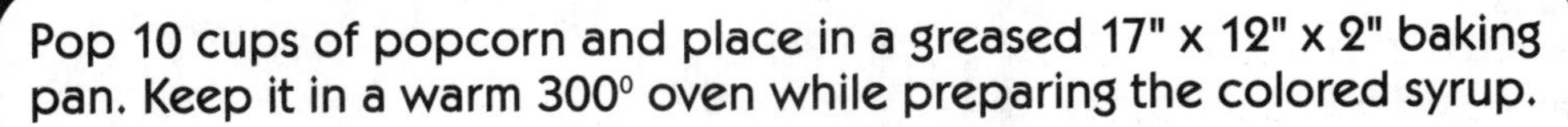

Pop 10 cups of popcorn and place in a greased 17" x 12" x 2" baking pan. Keep it in a warm 300° oven while preparing the colored syrup.

Grease the bottom and sides of a 2-quart saucepan. Combine 1 cup butter or margarine, 3/4 cup sugar, one 3-oz package of Jell-O™ (red or blue), 3 tablespoons water and 1 tablespoon of light corn syrup. Use a candy thermometer; cook and stir over medium heat until the temperature reaches 225° (hardball stage).

Pour the syrup over the popcorn and toss to coat. Bake this mixture in a 300° oven for 10 minutes, stirring at least once during the baking time. Transfer this popcorn to another cool pan. (Makes one color; repeat for a second color.)

Cool completely breaking the popcorn into clusters. Proceed to make another batch in the other color. Serve the popcorn in class or make "doggie bags" to take home.

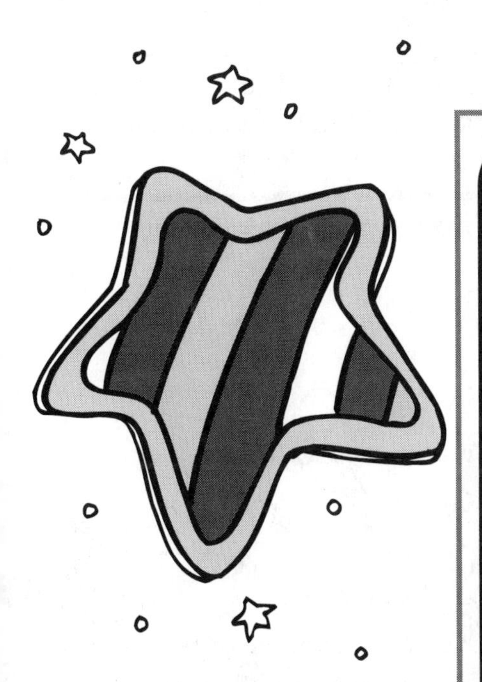

★ Patriotic Cookies ★

Ingredients

Use your own sugar cookie recipe, or try the one below.

⅓ c. soft margarine	⅓ c. sugar
⅔ c. honey	1 egg
1 tsp. vanilla	2 ¾ c. flour
1 tsp. salt	1 tsp. baking soda

Combine the first five ingredients and mix well. Add the remaining ingredients to form a dough. Chill overnight. The following day, roll out the dough and use cutters to make star or Uncle Sam hat shapes. Bake the cookie shapes for 8-10 minutes at 375°F. When the cookies cool, mix red and blue cookie paint by combining ¼ tsp. water and 1 egg yolk with a few drops of each food coloring. Have the children paint red and blue designs on their cookies using small new paintbrushes.

★ Patriotic Pattern Sticks ★

Ingredients
long, hors d'oeuvre toothpicks
strawberry chunks
blueberries or purple grapes
banana slices

Have the children slide the fruit onto the toothpicks in a specific sequence, such as one red strawberry, two white bananas, and one blueberry or grape.

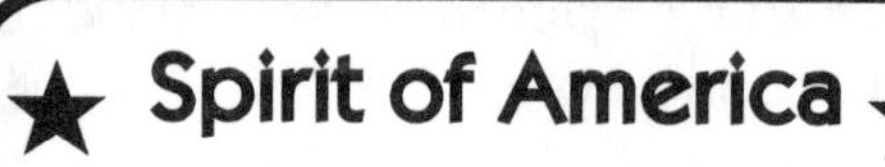

★ Spirit of America ★

Ingredients
graham crackers
cream cheese
blueberries
strawberries, chunked

Spread cream cheese over the graham cracker to make the flag background. Cluster several blueberries in the upper left-hand corner of the graham cracker to form a rectangle shape. Set strawberry chunks in rows across the rest of the cracker to form the red stripes. Space the red rows apart, leaving a white row between each.

★ Tempting Tents ★

Ingredients
ice cream cones
raisins
dry cereal shapes
fresh fruit chunks
peanut butter
nuts
sunflower seeds

Invert the ice cream cone and coat it with peanut butter. Decorate this tent with raisins, nuts, dry cereal shapes, sunflower seeds and fresh fruit chunks.

Statue of Liberty

This statue is made of caramel candies "glued" together by moistening each with water. Stack four caramels for the body. Cut half of a caramel for the head. For arms, cut a caramel in half and shape each piece into an arm (one holding a torch). Cut a crown from another candy caramel. Moisten these with water and sculpt this statue.

Firecrackers

Cover rolls of wrapped candy with crepe paper. Tie at each end with yarn; then fringe the paper. Glue on paper stars and stripes.

Patriotic Refreshments

Serve red, white and blue snacks to the children for added fun. Make pinwheel sandwiches with grape and strawberry jelly. Cut the edges from a slice of bread. Flatten the bread slightly with a rolling pin. Spread the filling and carefully form each slice into a roll. Cut the roll into bite-sized pieces. Serve red fruit punch with "blueberry bombs" (ice cubes). Place several fresh or frozen blueberries into each section of an ice cube tray. Freeze and serve these with the punch. Make star-shaped gelatin using molds and red or blue-flavored gelatin. Add a little whipped cream for a white topping.

Burst of Colors

Group eight plastic straws and tie them together at the center. Arrange the straws so they will stand up. Press large colored gumdrop candies onto the top of each straw.

Chocolate Treats

Chocolate Bread

Ingredients

1 c. sugar
3/4 c. chopped nuts
1 egg
1 tsp. allspice
1 1/4 c. orange juice
1 tsp. vanilla
3 c. biscuit mix
2 squares unsweetened chocolate
recipe makes 1 loaf

Combine the sugar and the egg. Add the orange juice and biscuit mix and blend thoroughly. Melt the chocolate squares in the top of a double boiler. Blend the melted chocolate, nuts, allspice and vanilla into the biscuit batter. Pour the mixture into a greased loaf pan and bake 50-60 minutes at 350°.

Chocolate Soda Creams

Ingredients

chocolate syrup
ice cream (vanilla or chocolate)
whipped cream
chocolate candy pieces
milk
club soda

Have each child place 2 T. of chocolate syrup and 1/4 c. of milk in a glass and stir. Add a scoop of ice cream, then pour in club soda until the glass is almost full. Top with whipped cream and a candy piece.

Cocoasicles

Ingredients
4 bananas, cut in half
2 T. honey
6 T. cocoa powder
½ tsp. vanilla
2 T. milk
craft sticks

Combine the honey, cocoa powder, milk, and vanilla in a bowl. Mix until smooth. Insert a craft stick into the flat end of each banana half. Let the children hold the stick as they roll their banana pops over the cocoa mixture. Place the pops on a tray covered with waxed paper and freeze them overnight.

Fudge Pops

Ingredients
1 pkg. cook-and-serve chocolate pudding mix (3.4 ounces)
3 cups milk (whole milk works best)
1/4 cup cup sugar
1/2 cup whipping cream, whipped
wooden sticks or plastic spoons

In a saucepan over medium heat, combine pudding, milk and sugar; bring to a boil. Cook and stir for 2 minutes. Cool for 30 minutes, stirring several times. Fold in whipped cream. Pour into molds or small paper cups. Freeze until partially frozen; insert wooden sticks or spoons into center of pops. Freeze until firm, about 3 to 4 hours. Makes 13.

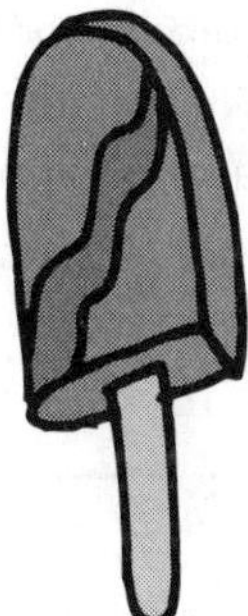

Chocolate Yogurt Pops

Ingredients
1 (16 oz.) container vanilla yogurt
4 T. cocoa powder
4 T. brown sugar

Place yogurt in a blender. Add cocoa and sugar. Liquify, then pour into small cups. Cover each cup with aluminum foil. Insert a craft stick through the foil into the yogurt mixture and freeze.

Melt-in-Your-Mouth Fudge

Ingredients

$1/2$ c. butter/margarine
$1/3$ c. boiling water
$4\,1/2$ c. powdered sugar
$1/2$ c. nonfat powdered milk
$1/2$ c. unsweetened cocoa powder
a pinch of salt
$1/2$ c. chopped nuts (optional)

Stir the butter into the boiling water until melted. Add the powdered sugar, powdered milk, cocoa powder and salt. Mix with a wire whisk or electric mixer until smooth. Stir in the nuts, if desired. Pour the mixture into a buttered 8" x 8" square pan and refrigerate several hours or overnight. Cut into 1" squares.

Moo Cookies

Heat oven to 375°F. In a large bowl beat butter with mixer til creamy. Add 1 cup of sugar until fluffy.

Beat in one egg and 1 teaspoon vanilla. Stir in $1/2$ cup dairy sour cream.

In a separate bowl, stir together $1\,3/4$ cups flour, $1/2$ teaspoon baking soda, $1/2$ teaspoon salt. With mixer on low speed, gradually add flour mixture to butter mixture, beating til well mixed.

Divide dough in half. Stir 1 ounce unsweetened (melted and cooled) chocolate into one half of dough. (If dough is sticky, cover and chill in the refrigerator about 30 minutes.) To form cookies, drop a teaspoon of white dough next to a teaspoon of chocolate dough. Bake 12 minutes.

Great Grahams

Jelly Graham

Ingredients
graham crackers, whole
strawberry jam
letter-shaped cereal
small candy conversational hearts

Have the children spread jam over their graham crackers. Let them spell their names across the jam with letter-shaped cereal; then place a candy heart "stamp" in the upper right-hand corner.

Initial Grahams

Ingredients
graham crackers, whole
chocolate chips
peanut butter

Have the children spread peanut butter over their graham crackers. Let them use the chocolate chips to write their initials in the peanut butter.

Chocolate Pudding Graham Cracker Cake

Ingredients
1 box graham crackers (recipe calls for 2 grahams per child)
1-2 packages chocolate pudding (regular or instant)
whipped cream and maraschino cherries

Arrange one layer of graham crackers on a large plate or tray. Prepare chocolate pudding mix according to package directions. Spread half of pudding mix onto graham crackers. Top with another layer of graham crackers and balance of pudding mix. Chill in refrigerator for one hour. Top each graham cracker squares with whipped cream and a cherry. Cut into individual squares and serve.

Favorite Summer Recipes

As you find new recipes, cut and attach them to this page for future use.

Name ______________________________

Summer Picnic

Number the pictures to show what you do first, second, third, then last. Then color the pictures, cut them out and staple them together in order to make a picnic book.

by Kim Rankin

Fill the Basket

Give each child a copy of the basket page and the fruit page.
Name fruits. Ask children to tell which fruit is their favorite.
Children color and cut out the fruits; then arrange them in the basket.
Display on a summer-theme bulletin board.

Creative Kitchen

Dear Parents,
These simple-to-make recipes will be ideal for you to prepare with your child at home. Each one ties in with a holiday, season, or special food.

September

Sweeten your child's taste for vegetables during National Honey Month in September with a simple recipe for honey gold carrots. Have your child help wash and chop about a pound of carrots. Boil the carrots in 3/4 cup of water until tender. Drain the carrots, add a tablespoon of butter or margarine, then drizzle with a tablespoon of honey. Stir to coat the carrots with the butter and honey. Serve warm.

October

October is Popcorn Poppin' Month. Celebrate with a taco-flavored snack recipe that's fun and easy to make. In a large pot, cook 1 cup of popping corn in 1/3 cup vegetable oil. After removing the popped corn from the heat, pour half of it into a large paper bag. To this bag, add one 1-oz. package of taco seasoning mix and 1 1/2 cups of unsalted peanuts. Pour in the remaining popcorn, fold over the top of the bag, hold tightly and shake to combine the ingredients.

November

Invite your child to make a tasty contribution to the Thanksgiving table. For this simple cranberry relish recipe, you will need 4 c. cranberries, 1 large orange, 2 c. sugar, and a food processor or blender. Leave the peel on the orange and cut the orange into pieces. Have your child measure the cranberries and sugar into the blender or food processor; then drop in the orange pieces. Finely chop the mixture. Empty the mixture into a bowl. Stir in 1/2 c. chopped walnuts, if desired. Cover and refrigerate for at least three hours. Garnish with mint leaves to serve (optional).

Creative Kitchen

December

'Tis the season to make hot cocoa. It will taste even better when you make your own mix. To make a personal cup of hot cocoa, place $\frac{1}{3}$ c. powdered milk, 1 tsp. cocoa powder, and 1 tsp. sugar into a large cup. Stir in one cup of hot water. Add mini marshmallows and/or red cinnamon candies and stir to dissolve. If needed, add cold water or milk to cool cocoa.

January

Here's an unusual outdoor activity that lends itself nicely to an indoor cooking experience. Open a fresh bag of large marshmallows. Have your child separate the marshmallows into two equal piles. Return one pile to the plastic bag. Take the second pile outside for a game of marshmallow hide and seek. Have your child hide his or her eyes while you hide the marshmallows in the snow. Let your child search the snow for the marshmallows. After finding the marshmallows, return to the kitchen to mix up a batch of hot cocoa mix. Have your child help measure $1\frac{2}{3}$ c. powdered milk, 1 c. powdered sugar, $\frac{1}{3}$ c. cocoa powder, and $\frac{1}{2}$ tsp. salt into a bowl or jar. Stir to mix well. Heat some water to boiling; then add two or three teaspoons of the cocoa mix to each cup of water. Add a few marshmallows from the bag. Store the remaining cocoa mix in an air-tight container for use at another time.

February

Warm up your kitchen this February with a quick and delicious cobbler in observance of National Cherry Month.

Quick Cherry Cobbler

Combine one 21 oz. can cherry pie filling with 2 tsp. lemon juice in a small bowl. Pour into an 8" square baking dish and spread evenly. Mix 1 c. biscuit mix with $\frac{1}{4}$ c. butter or margarine in a separate bowl, then add 3 T. boiling water and stir until a dough forms. Spoon dough over cherries. Combine $\frac{1}{4}$ c. granulated sugar with 1 tsp. each of cinnamon and nutmeg. Sprinkle this over the dough. Bake 25 to 30 minutes at 400°F until golden brown. Top dessert with softened vanilla ice cream for a special treat.

Creative Kitchen

March

In honor of St. Patrick's Day and the color green, create log snacks using celery stalks as "logs." Let your child experiment with creative celery stuffing using favorite foods. Start with the following examples; then fix up a few of your own ideas. 1. Mash a few slices of banana. Combine the mashed banana with a little peanut butter. 2. Stir a little crushed pineapple (drained) into a small amount of cottage cheese. Add a few finely chopped walnuts. 3. Combine peanut butter with a few crushed potato chips for extra crunch. 4. Stir a little granola and a few raisins into soft cream cheese. 5. Combine peanut butter and jelly with a little marshmallow creme. Stir until smooth. 6. Dice pieces of cucumber and apple. Stir them into cottage cheese.

April

Measure, mix, and chill a no-bake raisin snack for April.

Peanut Butter-Raisin Grahams

1 c. peanut butter
1/4 c. raisins
1/3 c. powdered milk
1/4 c. graham cracker crumbs
1/4 c. honey
1/2 c. flaked coconut
1/4 c. sesame seeds

Combine all of the ingredients in a large bowl, reserving some of the coconut. Roll the mixture into small balls, then into coconut. Chill and store in the refrigerator.

May

This May, during Pickle Week (third week in May), introduce your child to various types of pickles with a delightful Pickle Face Salad. You will need leaf lettuce, cottage cheese, sliced tomato, bread and butter pickle slices, dill pickle spears, and sliced baby gherkins. Have your child set a lettuce leaf on a plate. Top the lettuce with a mound of cottage cheese for a head. Add baby gherkin slice eyes and a nose. Cut a tomato slice into a half circle for a mouth. Place a dill spear across the top of the cottage cheese for a hat brim and build a hat above this with bread and butter pickle slices. Finish off with bread and butter pickle ears. To eat, scoop up cottage cheese with pickle pieces, or use a fork or spoon.

Simple Summer Snacks

Super Simple Snacks

Snack activities are suitable for all ages. Activities such as these enhance vocabulary development and sequential order, as well as encourage children to make use of measurement. "Cone"wich: Have your child assist you in making egg, tuna or chicken salad. Let your child scoop some of this sandwich salad into an ice cream cone for a delicious, nutritious treat. For an Independence Day treat, try making three separate bowls of sandwich spread. Add food coloring to the mayonnaise to make one bowl red and one bowl blue, leaving the third bowl white.

Creative Kitchen

Invite your child to create a few cool concoctions for summertime snacks.

Raspberry Cooler

1 pint raspberry sherbet
½ c. chilled cranberry juice

Place the sherbet in a blender container. Add the cranberry juice and blend until soft and smooth. Makes four servings.

Cheese Bumblebees

cracker shapes—circles or ovals, triangles
cream cheese
black string licorice
yellow food coloring

Tint the cream cheese with the food coloring. For each bee, spread yellow cream cheese over one circle or oval and two triangle crackers. Place the rounded cracker on a plate as the bee body, and place the triangle wings at either side. Cut or rip black licorice antennae and stripes for the bee's body. Place these appropriately.

Sunny Sherbet Shake: With your child's help, measure 1 cup of vanilla yogurt, 1 cup of orange sherbet and 1 cup of sliced peaches into a blender. Blend, then pour into a plastic container. Let your child count and add three or four ice cubes. Seal the container tightly with its lid and have your child shake the drink. While the drink chills for a few minutes, let your child color an American flag on a small piece of paper. Tape this flag near the top of a drinking straw. Now, pour the shake into a favorite glass or mug, add the straw, sip and enjoy.

Vocabulary Boosters

Use these words associated with preparation and cooking to increase your students' vocabulary. Ask children to describe what has been done to encourage them to use the new words and terms.

bake: cook in the oven

beat: mix very fast with a spoon or electric mixer

blend: mix ingredients together thoroughly so they are smooth

boil: cook in liquid that is bubbling and steaming

broil: cook by direct heat, usually under a heating unit in an oven

brown: cook in oil or butter over medium heat until ingredients turn brown

chill: place in refrigerator until thoroughly cold

chop: cut into irregular pieces with a knife, chopper, or food processor

combine: mix ingredients together thoroughly

cool: allow to come to room temperature

cream: mix ingredients together until soft

cube: cut into pieces about 1/4" to 1/2" on all sides

dice: cut into small pieces of the same size

dot: scatter bits of an ingredient over the top of food

drain: pour off liquid

fold: gently add an ingredient to a mixture by turning over

fry: cook in hot shortening or oil

garnish: decorate by placing pieces of colorful food on the top and sides of a dish

grate: cut into tiny particles using small holes of a grater

pare: cut off outer covering with a knife or other sharp tool (apples, cucumbers, potatoes, etc.)

peel: strip off outer covering (oranges)

refrigerate: place in refrigerator to store

shred: cut into thin pieces using large holes on grater or shredder (shredded foods look like strips)

simmer: cook in liquid just below the boiling point

stir: combine ingredients with circular motion to a uniform consistency

whip: beat rapidly in order to incorporate air

Cooking Utensils to Have on Hand

Here's a working list of utensils to keep in class so you'll always be ready to cook and create with your kids. Send a copy of this list home with children asking parents to donate items for use in your classroom.

plastic mixing bowls in various sizes
wooden mixing spoons
spatula
flat, dull spreading knives
sharp knife with protective sleeve for cutting
plastic spoons, forks, and knives
measuring cups
measuring spoons
cookie sheets
food coloring
cupcake tins
wire whisk
pot holders
pots and pans
cookie cutters
rolling pin
grater/shredder
dishwashing detergent
cutting board
waxed paper
paper towels
paper plates and cups
plastic spoons, knives, and forks
cupcake liners

Safe Cooking Rules

Cooking is a fun activity, but there are several safety tips you should always follow. Follow these rules and tips to be assured of a safe cooking environment.

Around the Stove and Oven

- Always get your parent's permission before you use the oven or stove.
- Don't walk away from, or turn your back on, a frying pan cooking with oil.
- Never fry oil at a high temperature.
- When using an oil cooking spray, don't spray over the stove or near heat. Spray over the sink or on the countertop.
- Always use pot holders or oven mitts when handling something hot. Do not use wet pot holders. These will send the heat from the hot item you are holding directly to your skin.
- Avoid wearing shirts with long and baggy sleeves as they could catch fire.
- Avoid overfilling pots or pans with boiling or simmering liquids.
- Keep handles of pots and pans turned away from the edge of the stove top.
- When opening lids on heated pots or pans, open the lid away from you and others so steam can escape safety.
- Use long-handled spoons when stirring hot liquids and foods.
- Never use water to put out a pan fire containing oil. Water will make the fire worse. Smother the fire by covering it with a pan lid, or pour baking soda on the fire.

Using a Microwave Oven

- Use only cookware and paper products that are microwave-safe.
- Use pot holders to remove items.
- If a dish is covered, be sure there is some opening for the steam to escape during cooking.
- When removing cooked foods from the microwave, open the container so that steam escapes away from you or others standing close by.
- Prick foods such as hot dogs and potatoes with a fork before placing them in the microwave.
- Do NOT cook a whole egg in a microwave as it will burst.
- Use the microwave only if you know exactly how to use it!

Handling and Using a Knife

- Pick up a knife only by its handle.
- Pay close attention to what you are cutting and don't look away.
- Always cut away from your body and away from anyone nearby.
- Avoid leaving a knife near the edge of a counter or table.
- Don't leave a knife where a small child can easily reach it.
- When cutting or slicing with a knife, use a sliding, back-and-forth motion.
- Avoid trying to catch a falling knife.

Measuring Tips

In cooking, ingredients can be measured three different ways.

- Items can be counted (three lemons).
- Items can be measured by weight ($^1/_2$ lb. of apples).
- Items can be measured by volume ($^1/_2$ lb. of sugar).

When measuring the volume of dry ingredients such as sugar or flour, spoon the ingredient into a measuring cup and level it off with a flat table knife. Avoid packing the cup. DO NOT press down to make room for more unless the recipe says to do so.

When measuring the volume of liquids, always put the measuring cup on a flat surface so you can easily see it at eye level. Check to see that the liquid goes up to the proper line on the measuring cup.

Measuring Equivalents

1 tablespoon = 3 teaspoons

1 cup = 16 tablespoons

1 cup = 8 fluid ounces

1 quart = 2 pints

1 quart = 4 cups

1 quart = 32 fluid ounces

1 gallon = 4 quarts

1 stick of butter or margarine = $^1/_2$ cup = 8 tablespoons

Creative Cooking Certificate

awarded to

Junior Chef

---

for following safe cooking rules
and for following directions.

Teacher

CRANBERRIES

Cooking Extenders

It's never too early to begin to expand children's learning horizons. We hope the joys of cooking in this compilation will give the children in your class a new interest and awareness in learning about and preparing foods.

Here are some additional ways to bring the pleasures of cooking into the classroom while also involving cooperation with the community and parents at home.

- Tune in to cooking shows on television while at school and view the program as a class. Afterwards, name the ingredients and discuss new cooking terms to add to children's vocabulary.
- Make a list of different cooking shows on television including the local channels and viewing schedule. Send the list home as a guide for parents. This can awaken an interest in parents' viewing as it encourages new interests in children and serves as quality family viewing time.
- Encourage children to bring in easy recipes they may have helped with at home. Try these in class. Add them to a class cookbook.
- Invite parents with culinary skills to come to class to demonstrate and cook a special dish or bake a treat.
- Arrange to visit a local restaurant, bakery, or confectionery to see chefs and bakers create and decorate.
- Invite a local chef or baker to come to class to talk about their work.
- Set up a library in class with children's cookbooks and recipes. Include kitchen items for role-playing and dramatization.